LETTERS TO A
Young
CALVINIST

LETTERS TO A
Young
CALVINIST

An Invitation to the Reformed Tradition

James K. A. Smith

BrazosPress

a division of Baker Publishing Group
Grand Rapids, Michigan

Published by Brazos Press
a division of Baker Publishing Group
P.O. Box 6287, Grand Rapids, MI 49516-6287
www.brazospress.com

Printed in the United States of America

Library of Congress Cataloging-in-Publication Data
Smith, James K. A., 1970–
    Letters to a young Calvinist : an invitation to the Reformed tradition
/ James K. A. Smith.
      p.   cm.
    Includes bibliographical references.
    ISBN 978-1-58743-294-1 (pbk.)
    1. Reformed Church—Doctrines. 2. Imaginary letters. 3. Calvinism.
I. Title.
BX9422.3S65 2010
230'.42—dc22
                                                      2010023575

In keeping with biblical principles of creation stewardship, Baker Publishing Group advocates the responsible use of our natural resources. As a member of the Green Press Initiative, our company uses recycled paper when possible. The text paper of this book is comprised of 30% post-consumer waste.

For
David, Frank, Myra, Sherryl, Carlos, Cheryl,
and Danny

This I pray, that your love might increase more and more in knowledge and true discernment, so that you might discover the things that really matter, in order to be pure and blameless until the day of Christ.

Philippians 1:9–10 (author's translation)

Contents

Contents

Introduction

Who would have guessed that in our postmodern culture something as austere as Calvinism would be both hip and hot? Quite apart from the five-hundredth anniversary of John Calvin's birth in 2009, over the past several years what has been described as the "new Calvinism" has generated increasing interest and devotees—chronicled most fully in Collin Hansen's journalistic account, *Young, Restless, Reformed: A Journalist's Journey with the New Calvinists*. Associated with noted pastors such as John Piper and Mark Driscoll—as well as scholars such as Al Mohler and D. A. Carson—attention to the new Calvinism reached a crescendo when *Time* magazine, in an admittedly curious claim, designated it as one of the "Ten Ideas Changing the World Right Now" (March 12, 2009).

I experienced some of this newfound interest in Calvinism in an unlikely place: an Assemblies of God church in inner-city Los Angeles. While my wife and I served as directors of the college and career ministry at Del Aire Assembly of God in Hawthorne, California (which is a long way from *Bel* Air, just to clarify!), I witnessed an increasing hunger for rigorous theological reflection amongst the (mostly Latino/a) twenty-somethings in our group. Looking to develop Christian minds with theological depth, and casting about for an intellectual tradition they couldn't find in their Pentecostal heritage, these young people, not surprisingly, were attracted to the riches of the Reformed tradition. Anecdotally, this seems to be a common trajectory for many evangelicals.

Indeed, this is my own story. I was converted and formed through an evangelical tradition marked by a strange kind of biblicist yet antitheological atmosphere that engendered a generally anti-intellectual ethos. But then I discovered the Reformed tradition of "Old Princeton" while in Bible college—the rich theological heritage of Princeton Theological Seminary in the nineteenth century (helpfully outlined in Mark Noll's anthology, *The Princeton Theology*). I can still remember an all-nighter that I spent immersed in the works of Charles Hodge, B. B. Warfield, and W. G. T. Shedd. I drank in their wisdom and erudition with an almost giddy sense of excitement and renewal, constantly whispering to myself, "Where have you been my whole life?" It was as if I had finally discovered why I had a brain.

Having dived into this deep river of theological reflection, it didn't take long for me to begin devouring the work of more contemporary authors such as Francis Schaeffer, J. I. Packer, and John Piper, who in turn pointed me *back* to giants like Augustine, John Calvin, John Owen, and Jonathan Edwards. In the Reformed tradition I found a home I've never left, even if I might now spend most of my time in other rooms of this sprawling estate that is "Calvinism."

However, in looking back at the enthusiasm of my younger, newly Calvinist self, I also cringe at the rough edges of my spiritual hubris—an especially ugly vice. The simple devotion of my brothers and sisters became an occasion for derision, and I spent an inordinate amount of time pointing out the error of their ("Arminian") ways. How strange that discovering the doctrines of grace should translate into haughty self-confidence and a notable lack of charity. I had become a caricature of the unforgiving servant in Jesus's parable (Matt. 18:23–35). At times, I saw creeping versions of the same pride in these young folks I spent time with in Los Angeles—an arrogance I understood but also abhorred. And in this particular case, there seemed to be something in their Calvinism that gave comfort to wider cultural notions of machismo that did not reflect the radical grace and mercy of the gospel. Calvinism became a sophisticated theological justification for patriarchal attitudes and practices. The collective shape of the "Calvinism" they had found was not pretty—and certainly not a winsome witness to God's coming kingdom. I sometimes encounter the same in the "new Calvinists" I bump into.

Looking back at my own enthusiastic induction into Calvinism, I can see another unfortunate aspect that often seems to characterize the "new Calvinism": my fascination with the Reformed tradition was largely truncated, fixated on issues of election and predestination and on parsing the arcane aspects of the acronym TULIP, which claimed to capture the so-called five points of Calvinism: total depravity, unconditional election, limited atonement, irresistable grace, and the perseverance (or preservation) of the saints. And while that fixation seemed to come with a swagger and confidence that was quick to dismiss other Christian traditions, it also failed to really plumb the depths of the Reformed tradition itself. If we imagine the Reformed tradition as a great, sprawling mansion, it was as if I entered through the door of "Calvinism" into an ornate foyer, but then became so fascinated with that particular room that I never ventured into other rooms. When you've spent time wandering through the wonders of the Biltmore Estate, the bedazzlement of the foyer is put in context. (The title of Daniyal Mueenuddin's story collection, *In*

Other Rooms, Other Wonders, seems suggestive in this respect.) Only later was I invited (well, pushed!) into other rooms where I began to appreciate the full richness not just of Calvinism but of the wider Reformed tradition.

These letters are meant to be just such an invitation. The "Jesse" to whom they are addressed is an amalgam of those young men and women from Los Angeles who re-energized my own interest in, and appreciation of, Calvin and Edwards and Kuyper. But "Jesse" is also a bit of a stand-in for my younger self, such that, in an important sense, these are a collection of letters to myself—not just what I wish I'd known then, but also the counsel I wish someone had offered me. They are, I hope, first and foremost pastoral. At least, that was their origin—the concern and counsel of a mentor and friend to a young person beginning to tread water in this deep river. The letters don't at all pretend to be a comprehensive introduction to the Reformed tradition, but I do hope they offer a certain "education" in the sense of Friedrich Schiller's *Letters on the Aesthetic Education of Man*: the process of inviting and inducting someone into a tradition by meeting them where they are and then walking alongside them. To stick with our mansion metaphor, then, I hope these are the letters of an enthusiastic tour guide—or maybe even the letters of a longtime resident of this great estate that is "Calvinism"—who is eager to show a new visitor the riches of the mansion that might otherwise have remained hidden and unappreciated.

But the interest and concern of these letters is not just theological information; it is also spiritual formation. I hope the letters reflect a pedagogical process of growth, slowly walking the reader from room to room without rushing too quickly. As such, it is important that the letters be read in order, since each letter presumes a context and an ongoing conversation. I imagine the reader being in a certain place, at a certain starting point. So these letters don't offer an apologetic defense of Calvinism, trying to defend it against all comers; rather, I envision the addressee of these letters as someone who has already become interested in this tradition and is looking for a guide into unfamiliar territory. In fact, I generally imagine that the addressee of these letters might be a very enthusiastic convert to a newfound Calvinism, and so the letters for the most part assume that interest (though I hope they also prove helpful for other readers who may be in a different place). But above all, I imagine this correspondence as a kind of apprenticeship at a distance between two friends. That foundation of friendship is crucial and is assumed as the context in which these missives are traded. And so, at times, the pastoral concern of the letters will require some tough love and honest critique, words of caution and even admonition. But I hope the reader will keep in mind that, at these moments, I envision myself writing to a friend. In fact, I'm also writing to myself as much as anyone. Herein lies a critique of my younger (and even my older) self.

Finally, while these letters are written as an invitation to the Reformed tradition, such an invitation can only be instrumental, a way station of sorts. For the fount and end of the Reformed tradition is God himself as revealed to us in Jesus Christ and present with us in the person of the Holy Spirit. In other words, these letters are an invitation to the Reformed tradition only because the Reformed tradition is itself an invitation into the life of God. In his fifth-century manual for preachers, *Teaching Christianity* (*De doctrina christiana*), Augustine notes how strange it would be if a traveler to a distant country became so enamored with his means of conveyance that he never got out of the boat, even though the whole purpose of the ship was to convey him to another shore. The Reformed tradition is a way, not a destination; it is a means, not an end; it is a way onto the Way that is the road to and with Jesus. It is a ship that conveys us to the shore of the kingdom of God and propels us to an encounter with the Word become flesh. These letters are just little brochures spreading the news about the journey.

Welcome to the Family

Dear Jesse,

It was such a treat to receive your letter and hear the things God is doing in your life. It's hard to believe it's been four years since we made our move to Grand Rapids. It seems like just yesterday that our "theology group" was gathered together in room 10 at the church. Remember how intense the conversation was on that last night when we were discussing open theism? When we next get together, remind me to tell you how important that conversation was in my own walk and my theological pilgrimage.

What was most intriguing about your letter was the news of your recent immersion in Reformed theology. I'll be honest with you: I'm not surprised, and I'm more than a little thrilled by the whole development. As you've already said, this represents the beginnings of a harvest whose seeds were planted while we were studying together. I was glad—and a bit relieved—to hear you say that you felt like you "discovered" the Reformed tradition for yourself, from your own engagement with Scripture. I wouldn't want you to feel like you had to conform to some intellectual mold that I had created.

Given where you and I came from—the charismatic side of the evangelical tradition—I can certainly see why you are so animated with such a plethora of questions! That the Reformed tradition gives birth to such baptized curiosity is, I think, one of the best testimonies of its spiritual vitality. I love the way you put it: the Reformed tradition has helped you to discover deep wells in Scripture that you didn't know were there before. Indeed, we might say that what the Reformed tradition offers is a kind of "witching rod" that helps you find some of the deep spots in God's self-revelation—pointing out the places where you need to go do the hard work of *digging*.

So it would be both a pleasure and an honor for me to help orient you to this new path of discipleship—the path trod by the likes of Martin Luther, John Calvin, and Jonathan Edwards. It will be fun for us to keep up this correspondence as you continue to plumb the depths of Reformed theology. And I definitely think there's good reason to carry this out in writing (aside from the fact that we're 2,500 miles apart). Putting down your thoughts and questions in writing will help you articulate the issues, express your doubts (don't be afraid of doubts!), and start to get a handle on Reformed faith and practice.

Let me encourage you to take some risks as you set out on this pilgrimage to deepen your faith and your relationship with Christ. Don't be afraid to ask hard questions. As I always said in our Sunday school class, God isn't scared of our questions. Indeed, I think it is one of the hallmarks of the Reformed tradition that it has a long history of encouraging curiosity about creation. (Remind me to talk later about Kuyper's Stone Lectures at Princeton over a century ago, especially his account of the Reformed tradition's role in the development of science.) Unlike some of the places you and I have been, which really discourage questioning in order to get people to toe the party line, the Reformed tradition has long encouraged a kind of holy intellectual riskiness.

And don't worry about sounding silly or ignorant—as if someone asking questions was supposed to already have the answer (which would make asking questions pretty stupid, wouldn't it?). Sometimes you'll hear fellow Christians using terms or talking about ideas that it seems like you should know and that you might be embarrassed to admit you don't. Don't be intimidated: we have to start where we are. Above all, know how much I love you, and please count on me to be your guide. Let me be your Samwise in this Frodo-like quest you're on.

I'll be looking forward to hearing your questions.

Strength to your arm,

P.S. I've included here for you a great little book, *Ecumenical Creeds and Reformed Confessions*, that collects both the early Christian creeds (the Apostles' Creed, the Nicene Creed, and the Athanasian Creed) and three key Reformed confessional documents: the Heidelberg Catechism, the Belgic Confession, and the Canons of Dort. We'll talk about these more later, but you might find it helpful in the next week to read through the Belgic Confession. It's a wonderfully evangelical summary of Reformed faith and practice.

On Religious Pride

Dear Jesse,

I'm glad to hear that you've connected with a group of fellow Christians who are also exploring the same questions as you. As with any aspect of Christian discipleship, the pilgrimage of faith should never be a private, solitary affair. There should be no Lone Rangers in the Christian life. To play on the analogy I hinted at last time, the most important lesson Frodo learned in his quest is that he could never have done it alone. So I hope your band of brothers and sisters will be a kind of Reformed fellowship of the ring (yes, I'll try to stop with the Lord of the Rings tropes! ☺).

But I must also admit, Jess, that the tone of your letter seems a little different somehow. In your first letter I sensed a sanctified excitement about a renewed engagement with the Lord in his Scriptures—a sense of a deepened relationship that was taking you back to the Word with new eyes and a reanimated joy. But the way you talk in this most recent letter seems more concerned with pointing out what's wrong with all of the other Christians around you—especially our friends at church. I'll be honest with you: it sometimes sounds like you think you've achieved some new secret knowledge, which somehow gives you license to mock those who don't have it. I hope you'll receive this in love, but I'm not very thrilled with your posture here.

I wonder: do you think this is something that stems from this new group of "Reformed brothers," as you put it?

Now is as good a time as any to warn you about one of the foremost temptations that accompanies Reformed theology: *pride*. And the worst kind of pride: *religious* pride (one of Screwtape's letters speaks quite eloquently about this). This is an infection that often quickly contaminates those who discover the Reformed tradition, and it can be deadly: a kind of theological West Nile virus.

I know this because I've been there; I know the feeling, and the temptation. Having come from the same anti-intellectual Christian background, when I discovered Reformed theology it was like coming over that crest on Sandpiper Street near LAX: you know, where all of a sudden the car crests the hill and the ocean seems to just explode across the horizon. It's like seeing the Pacific for the first time all over again. The water is so inviting you can't help diving in. And then you can't understand why the Christians around you aren't doing the same thing. You become puzzled that they're not seeing what you see. And slowly but surely you find yourself looking down your nose at them, treating them with something less than Christian charity—all the while becoming puffed up with the kind pride that stems from knowledge (as Paul puts it in 1 Cor. 8:1).

Indeed, despite this tendency amongst young Calvinists, humility should in fact be the primary Calvinist virtue. Consider what Calvin himself says in the *Institutes* (2.2.11): "A saying of Chrysostom's has always pleased me very much, that the foundation of our philosophy is humility. But that of Augustine pleases me even more: 'When a certain rhetorician was asked what was the chief rule in eloquence, he replied, "Delivery"; what was the second rule, "Delivery"; what was the third rule, "Delivery"; so if you ask me concerning the precepts of the Christian religion, first, second, third and always I would answer, "Humility."'" This is why I think only Scots Calvinists could have invented the great Calvinist spiritual discipline of golf, that most humiliating of all games. If you're ever feeling haughty, just go out and try to hit a 3-iron from deep rough. (Note: this can be a very "spiritual" way to justify four hours on the course. You'll thank me for this later.)

But more seriously: if you don't recognize the temptations of hubris early, the infection of religious pride soon spreads, and you'll find that Reformed theology is reduced to polemics—and the worst kind of polemics: directed only at other Christians. There's a legitimate place for polemics, but you need to be wise about picking your battles. And for the most part, battling other Christians should not be a very high priority. We can talk more about this later. Unfortunately, this is a common malady in the Reformed tradition, and we would do well to be honest about this up front (sort of like knowing your family's medical history helps you to be aware of what could happen to you). I recently read an enlightening—if also a bit disheartening—essay by John Frame called "Machen's Warrior Children." In this cautionary tale he chronicles the history of Reformed schisms, fights, and debates throughout just the twentieth century in America. The list includes twenty-one (!) areas of debate; and as he notes, this doesn't even include the full spectrum of issues (such as women in office, etc.). This type of polemical religious pride almost seems like a kind of genetic defect of the Reformed tradition, one that threatens to perpetuate itself.

Now, I may be wrong, but it sounds to me like the group of "Reformed brothers" that you speak of has a serious case of this infection. My hunch about this was confirmed when you told me that they were devotees of that radio program "Saints and Infidels." (As you know from our time together, I have very little good to say about talk radio, even Christian talk radio, which seems to be a kind of breeding ground for the most uncharitable, unchristian polemics—like stagnant water is a breeding ground for West Nile virus.)

The fact that a mentor like José has also expressed concern to you about this group (and program) will, I hope, give you reason to think carefully about this cadre of newfound friends. Of course, I want you to find sisters and brothers who will help you on this journey: nothing is more important for discipleship and theological maturity than good friends. But friends are something that you *choose*, and not all acquaintances are *good* friends. True friends are those who encourage in you the fruit of the Spirit. I fear that this group of people will bear only bitter (yea, poisonous) fruit.

I hope you don't think I'm being too hard on you. I love you enough to take the risk of you thinking that.

Choose wisely,

Proud to Be a Calvinist?

Dear Jesse,

I appreciate your honesty: I expected my last letter would make you upset. But I'm also glad that, when you took a breath, stepped back for a few days, and thought about it, you could see the danger I was worried about. Indeed, it is a testimony of your maturity in Christ to already see that tendency in yourself and to purpose in your heart not to go further down that road. I wish I had had that kind of maturity and self-knowledge when I was younger; it took me a long time to be free of the pride and self-righteousness that had infected me. Or I should rather say: it took me a long time to *begin* to be free from pride. But if you can imagine, I used to be even more arrogant than I am now! What made this particularly reprehensible was that it was my supposed "discovery" of the doctrines of grace in Reformed theology that was the basis for an ugly pride and condescension, particularly toward other brothers and sisters in Christ. The irony, of course, is that I was supposedly discovering the deep biblical truth that everything is a gift. "Where, then, is boasting?" (Rom. 3:27).

In my case, I think this stemmed from the fact that my initial immersion in the Reformed tradition was largely a private affair rather than something pursued in community. I came to the Reformed tradition through a strange back door; indeed, it might have been a trapdoor. As I've shared with you before, I was not raised in the church and became a Christian the day after my eighteenth birthday, through the influence of Deanna's family. (While I've gone on to be a philosopher and an academic, I was really *loved* into the kingdom, which is why I think I have always gravitated to Augustine's emphasis on love and Edwards's emphasis on the affections.) This was a radical conversion for me—not because I'd been a wanton, licentious frat boy, but because I had long planned on a life of self-sufficiency and wealth. My entire high school career I had been planning to be an architect. But when I became a Christian, I immediately sensed a call to something else, and all my best-laid plans were toppled and upended.

Much to my surprise (and my family's chagrin), I found myself at Emmaus Bible College in Dubuque,

Iowa, a tiny little school in the Plymouth Brethren tradition (the corner of Christendom through which I became a Christian). Surprisingly enough, it was at Emmaus that I was introduced to the Reformed tradition. I say "surprisingly" because, keep in mind, the Plymouth Brethren basically invented dispensationalism—the eschatological framework that later gave us the Scofield Study Bible, Dallas Theological Seminary, and the Left Behind series of novels. Dispensationalism is usually understood as a rival to the covenant theology of the Reformed tradition. Nonetheless, several of my professors had a habit of calling themselves "four-point Calvinists" and regularly invoked the likes of B. B. Warfield, Charles Hodge, A. A. Hodge, and W. G. T. Shedd in my theology courses. At first I was intrigued, and then I was hooked. In these voices from Old Princeton I found a rigor, depth, and even philosophical orientation that thrilled my soul and seemed to scratch itches I didn't even know I had before. I began to spend countless hours in the library drinking from these deep new wells. But it was as if the books stacking up around me functioned as walls of isolation, creating a fortress of solitude that was also a bastion of pride. How strange it is that we can become prideful about gifts and can seize possession of what's given as if it was somehow our accomplishment.

If my own experience suggests anything, it's that pride can swell in isolation, though it can also have its own mob mentality too. So I'll still be praying that

God will bring alongside you the kinds of friends who will be co-pilgrims with you. In fact, I must tell you that in the past couple years I've become convinced that perhaps nothing is so important for our walk with the Lord as good friends. I think God gives us good friends as sacraments—means of grace given to us as indices of God's presence and conduits for our sanctification. While "there is a friend who sticks closer than a brother" (Prov. 18:24), that same Friend sends us friends to help make his presence tangible and concrete. Nothing continues the incarnation like Christian friendship. It's what I miss most about being back in Los Angeles: our time spent together encouraging one another, "as iron sharpens iron" (Prov. 27:17). I'm glad we can still experience something of that in these letters.

Blessings,

Grace All the Way Down

Dear Jesse,

That's a tall order: to sum up Reformed faith in one word! I suspect that you're trying to bait me, expecting my answer to be a strange one: TULIP—that felicitous turn of phrase that both summarizes the key points of the Canons of Dort and invokes the provenance of Reformed theology in the tulip-infested Netherlands. I know you've already heard it put that way, but I would answer your challenge a little differently. In a word, Reformed theology is fundamentally about *grace*. Let me explain.

At its heart, Calvinism is simply a lens that magnifies a persistent theme in the narrative of God's self-revelation: that everything depends on God. Everything is a *gift*. This doesn't just apply to salvation—it's true of creation itself.

God created the world out of—and for—his pleasure, as an act of love. There's no hint of necessity or requirement here: God could have *not* created the world. The world exists (and is sustained) only because of God's sovereign action; and creation is still radically dependent on God's gift of existence (Col. 1:16–17). So we might say that grace goes "all the way down." To merely exist as a creature is to be dependent on the gift of existence granted by a gracious God: to be is to be graced. "In him we live and move and have our being," as Paul put it (Acts 17:28—quoting a philosopher, by the way).

This theology of radical grace is captured in one of Augustine's favorite verses, 1 Corinthians 4:7: "What do you have that you did not receive?" The answer, of course, is *nothing*; or, stated positively, everything we have is something we have received as a *gift*. So we have no reason to "boast," Paul says, as if anything was "ours" in the first place.

Now, usually when people get thinking about Calvinism, they're concerned about soteriology (that is, the doctrine of salvation). And the question, posed somewhat falsely, is something like: "Is salvation God's work or my own?" But when I say that Calvinism (or Reformed theology, or Augustinianism, or whatever you want to call it) is fundamentally about *grace*, I have intentionally pointed you back to creation in order to not get confused or sidetracked by just the soteriological question. If Calvinism has a radical understanding of the role of God's grace in salvation, that's simply an extension of its understanding of God's grace in creation. If one doesn't locate grace in creation, one could fall into the very problematic notion of thinking that God is *gracious* only because of and after the fall (we might have occasion to talk about this more later).

But, of course, this reality of grace going "all the way down" is equally true when it comes to the question of our salvation. God's revelation in the Scriptures indicates the radical *inability* of the sinner to "choose the Good" (as philosophers put it). In fact, the Scriptures describe the sinful human being as "dead" (Eph. 2:1), and, as you know, corpses have no abilities. In other words, the effect of sin is such that, while human creatures remain structured in such a way that they still desire God, that structure is perverted and misdirected toward aspects of the creation rather than toward the Creator (see Rom. 1:21–32). This creational structure—this desire for God—can only be properly *re*-directed by God himself. What this requires, then, is for God to restore and renew and, in a sense, *re-create* (2 Cor. 5:17). So when Paul continues in Ephesians 2, he chooses his words very carefully: because we were dead, and lacked the ability to choose God as our proper end, God "made us alive" (Eph. 2:4–6). Note that God is the actor in this sentence, not us. Because we were dead, it could only be "by grace" that we have been saved through faith, and that, we are told, is not of ourselves (Eph. 2:8). What does that mean? Very simply, salvation is a *gift*—and not just the "objective" work of Christ on the cross, but also the "subjective" appropriation of that work by faith: salvation *in its totality*. This has to be the case because, for a "dead" sinner, such faith is impossible. (Indeed, Paul tells us that for the "natural man"—that is, the unregenerate person—this whole matter is "foolishness" and cannot possibly be understood [1 Cor. 2:14].)

All of this is a testimony to God's grace, not only because it is a gift, but also because God *didn't have to do it*. As a Pascalian dictum so aptly puts it, "God owes us nothing." That's pretty close to a motto of Calvinism, to which I might add the correlative line: "Everything is a gift."

Well, it's getting late and the kids are still up. I've not answered all of your questions yet, but I'll send this off as a start. Stay tuned.

Peace,

P.S. Look again at Ephesians 2, which I quoted above. While many look to Ephesians 1 as a kind of classical passage for Calvinism (because of its talk of predestination), I think the core themes of Calvinism are better deduced from Ephesians 2.

17

God Owes Us Nothing

Dear Jesse,

You'll notice that in my last letter I managed to define the core of Calvinism without ever talking about election or predestination. That was intentional. I often feel that Reformed theology is ill served by a myopic focus on these themes, as legitimate as they are. But since these are clearly the topics you're most engaged by right now, let me try to map them onto the way I introduced the core of Reformed theology in my last letter.

You'll notice that while I identified grace as the heart of Reformed theology, this is intimately linked with a radical understanding of sin and the effects of the fall—"radical" insofar as it sees sin going to the very *roots* of our being (the Latin *radix* refers to "roots").

This is why in the Canons of Dort (as well as its popularization in the abbreviation TULIP), the question of "total depravity" comes first: it simply doesn't make sense to talk about "unconditional election" if one doesn't first appreciate the Bible's radical account of the fall and sin. So let me try to pick up where I left off last time.

If, as a Calvinist, I assert that the heart of the Christian story is *grace*, it might be that I was convinced of Calvinism because it took seriously the depths of sin. (But remember what I said last time: God didn't need the occasion of the fall or sin to be gracious. God simply *is* gracious, and creation itself was already an act of grace, an expression of love.) Sin is a corruption, distortion, and misdirection of our good creational structure. And that creational structure endures even in a fallen world. For instance, as I mentioned last time, God has created us to desire him. As Augustine so aptly puts it, "You have created us for yourself, and our hearts are restless until they rest in You" (*Confessions* 1.1.1). But that creational structure of desire—which can't be erased or obliterated—is fundamentally *mis*directed by sin. And more importantly, it cannot be properly *re*-directed by our own will (that's the core theme of book 8 of the *Confessions*). Therefore, the radical redirection of our will must be effected by God. This is usually summed up in the Reformed formula that "regeneration precedes faith"; that is, the renewing and re-creating work of the

Holy Spirit is the *condition* for my faith in Christ, not the *result* of it.

But, of course, this then raises the question: if God must first do the necessary work in order for my faith to be properly directed to Christ, then it seems clear that God does not do this in every person. And insofar as God is the free and sovereign Creator of the universe, it seems equally clear that no one could twist God's arm or bribe him to come do this work in their heart and will. (And, of course, given what we've said above, the unregenerate person couldn't even *want* this.) So it seems that God chooses who he will regenerate. That, in a nutshell, is the doctrine of election. God in his free and sovereign grace, and "for his own pleasure," as Edwards often puts it, chooses those on whom he will have mercy (Rom. 9:18). Those who are "chosen" are described as "the elect"—these chosen ones are "predestined" to salvation (Eph. 1:4–5).

The hard part of this answer to the question is its inverse: if God has chosen some to regenerate for his glory, then doesn't that mean he passes over many others? How is it fair for God to choose some as the objects of his re-creating grace, but not others? Indeed, why not all?

Let's not forget the principle we articulated last time: God owes us nothing. Gifts are not required, and God has no obligation to give. Of course, someone will respond: "So God can just choose to send people to hell?" That's not quite the right way to formulate the question: if God chooses to rescue some, that does not mean that he has thereby *caused* the condemnation of others. The most basic characteristic of sin is that it is *I* who am responsible for my sin: if I stand condemned, it is my fault. If I reap the punishment for that, it is still my fault. If someone else pays the fine for my cellmate, and he is released from his condemnation, my sin (and punishment) is still my fault.

The objector to this would be wiser to put the question this way: "If God is free to choose to regenerate *some*, why wouldn't a gracious, loving God freely choose to regenerate *all*?" Now that's a harder question. I'm tempted to invoke the perennial theological avoidance strategy and say "it's a mystery," but instead I'll just postpone that for a later discussion.

Is this helping? Let me know if I'm missing the mark. At this point, we should be worried about the forest, not the trees.

In Christ,

God Doesn't Even Owe Us an Answer

Dear Jesse,

OK, OK, I see your point. We quickly got to the 64-million-dollar question, and I punted. And I can appreciate that this is probably the hardest question your Arminian friends have put to you. So, while I'd like to postpone this until after we get a sense of the history of theology (especially some engagement with Saint Augustine and Jonathan Edwards), let's take a first shot at answering the question.

Looking back at my last letter, I see we formulated the question this way: "If God is free to choose to regenerate *some*, why wouldn't a gracious, loving God freely choose to regenerate *all*?" Now, in some ways, I think this is an unfair question, like the old loaded question: "Are you still beating your wife?" No matter how you answer the question, it's a losing situation. If I simply say no, then I've suggested that I *used* to abuse my wife. If I say yes, obviously I'm abusing my wife. The question is "loaded" because it forces the answerer to buy into a presupposition that may not be true.

Moreover, I do think that the question defies an answer insofar as it asks us to know the mind of God *as God knows himself*—which, of course, is impossible for finite human beings. In a real sense, there is a mystery at stake here, particularly since Scripture is so silent on these before-the-world-was-created kinds of questions (though, admittedly, a lot of Reformed folks seem to have thought they had insider info on what God was thinking before creation).

Nevertheless, refusing to answer the question will not satisfy your critics, nor even honest seekers. The question is very legitimate in one sense, and it arises from some of our deepest sensibilities about fairness, justice, and goodness. It expresses discomfort with the notion of God not helping those he could, somehow restraining his goodness. At the same time, I think the Calvinist answer calls into question just those sensibilities and presuppositions. If I were less charitable, I would say the Calvinist answer calls into question our notion of God as a kind of bubble gum dispenser of goods *for us*. The question is, in a certain sense, generated by a thoroughly anthropocentric view—a perspective that imagines that this is all about us (human beings), and therefore God has to give an account of why he does not dispense his grace to all. But a distinguishing mark of Calvinism—in worship, theology, and practice—is a decidedly *theocentric* perspective that sees the whole drama of creation, fall, and redemption as ultimately *about God*, and more specifically, God's glory. Contemporary evangelicalism, dominated by a kind of Arminian consensus, has become so thoroughly anthropocentric that it ends up making God into a servant responsible for taking care of our wants and needs. (Rodney Clapp calls this "Winnie-the-Pooh" theology, drawing on Pooh's logic: "I hear a bee buzzing; where there are bees, there is honey; and where there is honey, it must be *for me*.") But Calvinism offers a radically different worldview and requires a paradigm shift in our thinking, from a focus on our wants and needs to a focus on God's glory. "What is the chief end of man?" the Westminster Catechism asks. "To glorify God and enjoy him forever." However, the *Prayer of Jabez*–minded evangelicalism we're coming from (where preachers are more akin to Tony Robbins–like hucksters than to Puritan preachers) seems to say almost the opposite: "What is the chief task of God? To make me happy and give me what I want."

So, to come back to our hard question: the answer must also be hard. First, I don't know why God chooses some and not others. I'm not going to pretend that I do. Second, "God owes us nothing," which means that, in a way, he doesn't even owe us an account of why he chooses some rather than others. To think that God would *owe* us such an account would be to compromise the absolute freedom and sovereignty of God. If God were *obligated* to give an answer, then God would be in some way subservient to the creature, which would compromise his lordship as Creator. As Paul puts it, "Who are you, O man, who answers back to God? The thing molded will not say to the molder, 'Why did you make me like this,' will it?" Rather, the potter has a right over the clay (Rom. 9:20–21 NASB). Third, it remains the case that, as hard as it is for us to understand, God is and will be glorified by both the salvation of the elect and the condemnation of the damned (Rom. 9:22–23).

Finally, one important response to the Arminian critics you are engaging: they will tell you that Calvinism makes God an unloving tyrant, because he doesn't choose to save everyone. But your Arminian objector has a similar problem: unless she is a universalist (and I know she's not), then she clearly thinks that not all are saved. But she is always so eager to assert that "God is not willing that any should perish." Obviously, some (many?) do; so is God not *able* to accomplish his will? Does she think that God's will can be thwarted? Is God not sovereign and all-powerful (omnipotent)?

Now your Arminian friend will reply that God *freely chooses* to, in a way, limit his power in this regard because he wants to "respect" the free will of human beings. (You've heard that ridiculous line about God being a "gentleman," right?) Well, now we're back where we began: if, ultimately, your Arminian interlocutor thinks my salvation comes down to *me* making a decision "by my own free will," then we have two problems: (a) This doesn't seem to square with what the Scriptures say about the depth of the effects of sin on our will (and whole person). In short, it fails to appreciate that *sin* goes "all the way down," or at least right through everything. This, I think, is the most serious problem with the Arminian position. But also, (b) if it really comes down to me acting on the basis of my own will, then my salvation would seem to be, at least in part, my own doing. In other words, grace would not go "all the way down." On top of that, it would again put the Creator in the position of being at the behest of the creature, since the Arminian would have to say, "Well, yes, God *wants* you to be saved, but his will is constrained by what *you* choose to do." So the creature calls the shots while the Creator sits by hoping and praying that I'll come to the prom with him? Sounds like a demeaning picture of God to me.

That's a lot to chew on, I know. Let this percolate for a while and get back to me.

In his service,

P.S. I think it is Jonathan Edwards who best captures this sense of the centrality of God's glory. And perhaps the best restatement of this is found in John Piper's classic, *Desiring God*, which I can still remember reading when I was in college. When you get a chance, check out the book that brings the two of these together: in *God's Passion for His Glory*, Piper provides the text of Edwards's piece, *The End for Which God Created the World*, and then provides his own commentary on the text.

Semper Reformanda

Dear Jesse,

Let's be clear about one thing: please don't expect my letters to provide the magic bullet that will eliminate all your doubts, answer every question, and defeat all comers. I can understand why you might remain frustrated and a bit dizzied by our recent correspondence, but I would ask you to do two things: first, don't expect too much from me. I honestly still feel like a student on these matters, and your questions are teaching me as much as any of my answers might. Second, don't despair. We're just getting started in this conversation; you have a lifetime to grapple with your questions, fears, and doubts. And be forewarned: when you feel like you've dealt with your current anxieties and confusion, there'll be more to follow. I promise.

And that might not be all bad. My own relationship to the Reformed tradition has not been one of linear "rosiness." Further explorations in a wider Reformed orbit caused me some real angst and tears—to the point that there were times when I was ready to chuck the whole thing. Part of this was because of real shortcomings within the Reformed tradition, and part was due to the limited corner of the Reformed tradition with which I was familiar. Realizing both of these things meant working through what I inherited as pristine and unquestionable. In short, I had to unlearn some of what I had absorbed; but doing so actually helped me to reaffirm much. Having worked through some of those doubts and made my way through some of those detours, I've come back to the Reformed tradition with new eyes, and a new appreciation.

It seems to me very un-Reformed to prop up Reformed theology as a timeless ideal, a consummated achievement, when one of the Reformers' mantras was *semper reformanda*—always reforming. You shouldn't expect a lifetime of pursuing the truth to result in constant entrenchment into what you thought when you were twenty. Wouldn't you expect the Spirit to lead you to grow and change? Alasdair MacIntyre says that what makes a tradition a "tradition" is precisely that we fight over what counts as part of the tradition!

Sorry. I'm foisting my own middle-aged frustrations onto you. Suffice it to say that doubt, confusion, and questions are not the enemy. They pose no special threat to the Reformed tradition. Not all who wander are lost.

Faithfully,

P.S. Sorry, I just realized I forgot to answer your question! I'm intrigued that you are sensing a call to be a pastor or theologian. I'll certainly be praying for you as you discern this call. But you asked something more practical: What should you be doing to become a Reformed theologian? That's easy: teach third-grade Sunday school.

Jesse
4955 El Segundo Blvd.
Hawthorne, CA 90250

Postcard from Geneva

Greetings from Geneva! I couldn't resist the opportunity to send you a note from John Calvin's command center, as it were. I'm here for a conference that's taking place in the *Auditoire au Calvin*, the teaching hall adjacent to St. Pierre's Cathedral, where Calvin (and John Knox and Theodore Beza) preached. This was the epicenter of the Swiss Reformation. But it's also interesting to see and consider Calvin's impact on the city of Geneva. Calvin's "Calvinism" wasn't just a doctrine of salvation. It was a vision for all of life suffused and nourished by God's grace. When you're here, you have an appreciation that Calvin saw the Redeemer at work beyond individual souls—that redemption was as big as creation itself. Kind of makes you ask: *How big is your Calvinism?*

Adieu,

A Historical Tour of Reformed Theology

Dear Jesse,

My time in Geneva has got me in a historical state of mind. So let's change gears a bit and go back to questions you asked in your second letter, about the history and background of the Reformed tradition. This will also help us to avoid becoming completely mired in the soteriological aspects of Reformed theology (i.e., questions about election, predestination, and salvation). While this is what most people think of when they hear about "Calvinism," in fact it is a fairly small (though essential) slice of the bigger vision that is Reformed theology.

There are people who can do a much better job than I can of narrating the history of the Reformation. (I'd recommend Alister McGrath's engaging account in *Christianity's Dangerous Idea*.) I'll give you just a thumbnail sketch, with a specific focus on the history of Reformed *theology*. While it is dated, I think it would still be very helpful for you to look at a number of the essays collected in B. B. Warfield's *Studies in Theology*, including the essays on Luther's Ninety-five Theses and others on the development of Reformed theology in Calvin and later.

We celebrate Reformation day on October 31, commemorating the day in 1517 when Martin Luther, an Augustinian monk, nailed his famous Ninety-five Theses on the door of the church in Wittenberg (Germany). This was a call for debate, protesting what Luther saw as a degeneration of orthodox Christian theology in the late medieval church. So this was a *protest* that called for *reform*: hence the appellation "Protestant Reformation." There were both earlier and later rumblings of the same themes in Jan Hus, William Farel, and John Calvin—a Frenchman who eventually landed in (or was dragged to) Geneva.

Now originally, the Reformers were really about reform, not schism, but given the extremity of their stance (proportionate to the extremities of both late medieval corruption and the counter-Reformation's response), this ultimately issued in new churches—or new branches of the church, we might say. So out of the Reformation arose the Lutheran churches (shepherded especially by Luther's successor, Philipp Melanchthon), and then churches whose origins were closer to Calvin. Some elements of the Reformation also took hold in England, leading to the emergence of Anglicanism. (The Anglican Articles of Religion, often called "The Thirty-Nine Articles," is quite a powerful statement of Reformed theology. Would that more Episcopalians actually believed it today!) Some of the most exciting work in historical theology over the past decade has concerned what is called "post-Reformation" theology, or sometimes "Protestant scholasticism." This involves the development of Reformed theology in the seventeenth and eighteenth centuries, particularly in continental Europe, in the work of people like Francis Turretin. My colleague at Calvin Seminary, Richard Muller, is the guru in this area.

Calvin's vision for Reformed Christianity especially took root in the Netherlands and Scotland, giving us two distinct but related streams of Reformed theology and practice. Arising out of the Netherlands would come a strain of theology most generally described as "Dutch Reformed." (This was also the faith of some of the earliest American settlers who founded New Amsterdam, which is why the Reformed Church in America is the oldest denomination with a continuous ministry in this country.) It is this side of the Reformed tradition that gives us some of the most significant Reformed creeds and confessions: the Belgic Confession, the Heidelberg Catechism, and the Canons of Dort. Dutch Reformed theology would later be articulated by Abraham Kuyper, Herman Bavinck, and Louis Berkhof. It would also be the stream that produced folks like Richard Mouw, Alvin Plantinga, and Nicholas Wolterstorff—names that I hope will become more familiar to you. Today this side of the tradition would be linked to institutions such as Calvin College and Seminary and, to a lesser extent, the Free University of Amsterdam (as well as institutions in Canada, South Africa, and Indonesia). And it is the tradition that informs denominations such as the Christian Reformed Church, the Reformed Church in America, and the United Reformed Church, a recent offshoot of the Christian Reformed Church. (If John Frame can write of "Machen's warrior children," Abraham Kuyper has his share of warring children as well.)

Through the influence of John Knox, Scotland gave birth to another stream of Reformed theology, crystallized by the Westminster divines in the Westminster Confession and the Larger and Shorter Westminster Catechisms. It is this Anglo-Scottish stream that would give rise to Puritans like John Owen, Richard Baxter, and, later in the colonies, Jonathan Edwards. This strain of Reformed theology would eventually be articulated in America in Old Princeton, and would be associated with figures we've met already: Charles Hodge, B. B.

Warfield, and A. A. Hodge. Today it would be associated with Westminster Theological Seminary (founded by some who left Old Princeton in 1929), Reformed Theological Seminary, and Covenant Seminary, but it also seems to play a surprising role at places like Southern Baptist Theological Seminary. (More on that "surprising role" some other time.) Denominational expressions of this stream would include the Presbyterian Church in America (PCA) and the Orthodox Presbyterian Church (OPC), as well as the "mainline" denomination, the Presbyterian Church (USA).

What's perhaps surprising is how little these two streams—the Dutch and Scottish—seem to cross. (In the vein of Tertullian's famous question, "What hath Athens to do with Jerusalem?" we might ask: What hath Amsterdam to do with Edinburgh? Or what hath Grand Rapids to do with Philadelphia?) Once in a while there's a confluence. The great biblical scholar Geerhardus Vos began in Grand Rapids and ended up in Princeton; Cornelius Van Til's "presuppositionalism" seemed to be forged at the intersection of the two; Francis Schaeffer's cultural critique owed something to both; and Michael Horton is able to swim in both streams. But for the most part, unfortunately, these two traditions seem to pass as ships in the night.

I think this historical tour is important to help you situate your own entrée into the Reformed tradition: the Calvinism you've discovered flows from a (largely) Scottish source and bears the imprint of Old Princeton. It's the same portal through which I entered the sprawling tradition that is Calvinism. But I hope "zooming out" might help you appreciate that the Reformed tradition is bigger than Scottish Calvinism—indeed, *Calvin* is quite a bit bigger than Scottish Calvinism.

I'll look forward to hearing from you. And since this comes so close to your birthday, I'm enclosing a treat: George Marsden's magisterial biography of Jonathan Edwards. Enjoy!

Yours,

Augustine, Patron Saint of the Reformers

Dear Jesse,

I'm glad you enjoyed the little history lesson in the last letter: sort of a "history of the Reformed tradition for dummies." Not that you're . . . well, you know.

But I fear I might have slightly skewed the picture by not going back far enough. While we started with Luther, perhaps the central character in the Reformation was a theologian who came a millennium earlier: Saint Augustine. Luther, you'll recall, was a monk. And he was a monk in the Augustinian order, so it's not surprising that his vision of renewal was spawned by a new appreciation for the "Doctor of Grace."

(When I was at Villanova, a university run by the Augustinian order, I used to tease my Catholic colleagues by pointing out to them my sympathies with Martin Luther, *OSA*—from the "Order of Saint Augustine," their own order!) Calvin had been deeply impressed by the Renaissance humanism of people like Erasmus, and thus he saw the past as a source of renewal for the present. The "back to the sources" motto of humanism (so different from the chronological snobbery of the Enlightenment) is what turned Calvin's eye to the church fathers, and Augustine in particular. (Anthony Lane's book *John Calvin: Student of the Church Fathers* is immensely helpful for appreciating this point.)

It is Augustine who is really the patron saint of the Reformation—and only because the Reformers saw Augustine's theology as a powerful expression of a robustly *Pauline* theology. So without wanting to sound overly pious or triumphant, I think it is very important to see that "Reformed theology" was not a sixteenth-century invention. It was a recovery and rearticulation of a basically *Augustinian* worldview, which was itself first and foremost an unpacking of Paul's vision of what it meant that Christ is risen. So the pedigree of Reformed theology is much older than the 1500s and ultimately traces back to the New Testament witness. (In fact, it goes back even further than that, insofar as the Reformed notion of "covenant" provides a lucid, coherent way to make sense of the entirety of Scripture as *one* unfolding narrative rather than a series of discrete epochs or "dispensations." But we'll have to return to that theme later.)

This means that the Reformers did not simply see themselves as leaping back to the first century, or naively retrieving some sort of "pure" biblical perspective in contrast to tradition. While, of course, they would emphasize *sola Scriptura*, that did *not* mean for them a rejection of "tradition." Especially for Calvin, the tradition—particularly as articulated in the church fathers (like Augustine)—was an indispensable gift of wisdom for understanding God's revelation in his Word. While the tradition was subservient to the Word, the interpretive tradition of the church was a gracious partner and reliable guide. The role of Augustine in the Reformation is a clear indicator of this. Calvin would have thought it a foolish spurning of the Spirit's gifts to try to leapfrog over all he had shown to his servant Augustine. (D. H. Williams provides a very helpful, accessible discussion of this in *Evangelicals and Tradition*.)

This is why Luther and Calvin still understood themselves to be "catholics." While they might have been railing against the abuses of Roman Catholicism, they also understood themselves to be heirs of the catholic, universal, orthodox faith. In fact, I think we can best understand the Reformation as an Augustinian renewal movement within the church catholic. So, in a way that might be surprising, to be Reformed is to be catholic.

Traditionally yours,

Jesse
4955 El Segundo Blvd.
Hawthorne, CA 90250

Postcard from Princeton

Hey Jesse,

It's been quite a while since I've heard from you. I hope you're doing well. I'm just a bit concerned by your silence. Perhaps this card from Princeton will coax you out of being incommunicado. Here still stands Nassau Hall, the short-lived home of President Jonathan Edwards—who held the post for just two months before succumbing to smallpox. It's hard to imagine Edwards receiving much of a welcome in Nassau Hall today. How strange, too, to see his grave in the vicinity of that of his (in)famous grandson, Aaron Burr Jr. (Now I've got Gore Vidal's novel dancing through my head!)

Anyway, hope you're well. I look forward to hearing from you.

In hope,

J

To Be Reformed Is to Be Catholic

Dear Jesse,

Well, thanks for being frank and forthright. That takes some courage, and I appreciate it. And I can understand your concern. Seriously. I'm sorry that I perhaps sprung that on you a bit quickly and without sufficient explanation. I'm a little less thrilled with your friends who seem to have set themselves up as the arbiters of what (or *who*) counts as "Reformed," but I'll concede that I was perhaps moving a bit too fast. I owe you a better explanation.

But why the impatience, Jesse? Why is it that you think we're "getting off track"? Because we're not just talking about election and predestination? I'm trying to invite you to see that those themes are only a *slice* of Calvinism. Or perhaps we could say that Calvinism is just a "region" of Reformed theology; the map is much bigger than that.

Not even John Calvin considered those themes to be the indispensable heart of Reformed theology. My proof for that? Consider this: As Randall Zachman shows in his marvelous book *John Calvin as Teacher, Pastor, and Theologian*, Calvin was very much concerned with the formation of children in the Christian faith. (Imagine having John Calvin as your "children's pastor"!) In fact, this seemed to preoccupy him throughout his entire life of ministry, right up until the end, when he felt he still hadn't been successful—despite the fact that he had written two (very different) catechisms for children while pastoring in Geneva.

It's the difference between these two catechisms that I find interesting. The first catechism, written in 1537, is basically a template of what would later become his *Institutes*. Intended to help parents teach their children, it has the same structure as the *Institutes* and deals with many of the same topics. But after he returned to Geneva from his sojourn (exile) in Strasbourg, he realized the need to go back to the drawing board. The result was his 1545 catechism, which has a distinct pastoral feel and concern to "accommodate" itself to children in its pedagogy (for instance, using a question and answer format). Its opening question, anticipating the first question of the Westminster catechism, asks: "What is the chief end of human life?"

But what I find particularly notable is what Calvin *didn't* include. The catechism is focused on equipping children to grow into their profession of faith by training them and forming them for right *worship*—which *is* "the chief end of human life" (Augustine would say the same thing in book 19 of the *City of God*). And yet, in developing a program of formation to equip young people for "the chief end of human life," what themes does he drop from the 1536 catechism? He eliminates any discussion of free choice of the will, along with the doctrine of election and reprobation! Methinks John Calvin would have frustrated your Calvinist friends—so, in that respect, I feel like I'm in pretty good company. ☺

I note this only to situate the themes of election and predestination within the wider panoply of concerns that animated the Reformers. And this brings us back to the issue of being Reformed and being "catholic." While the doctrines of grace were certainly central to the Reformation's renewal of the church, these were part of a wider concern for reform. Keep in mind: the Reformers didn't just want to reform the doctrine of salvation (or the "doctrines of grace"); they were concerned with the renewal and reform of *the church*, and especially the church's *worship*. (Even more than that: Calvin was concerned about reforming the political life of Geneva, and a long legacy of folks in the Reformed tradition saw that the gospel had social implications. So the DNA of the Reformed tradition is replicated well beyond the doctrine of individual salvation. But we'll have to return to that at another time.)

My point here is that the Reformers were not revolutionaries; that is, they were not out to raze the church to the ground, get back to some "pure" set of New Testament church principles, and start from scratch. In short, they didn't see themselves as leapfrogging over the centuries of post-apostolic tradition. They were *re-form*ing the church. And in that respect, they saw themselves as heirs and debtors to the tradition that came before them. Indeed, they understood the Spirit as unfolding the wisdom of the Word over the centuries in the voices of Augustine and Gregory the Great, in Chrysostom and Anselm. To say the Reformed tradition is "catholic" is just to say that it affirms this operation of the Spirit *in history*, and thus receives the gifts of tradition as gifts of the Spirit, subject to the Word.

For folks like you and me—who've come to the Reformed tradition from primitivist backgrounds—I think this is one of the hardest things to absorb. By "primitivist" I mean Christian traditions that have a basically negative view of history and instead see themselves as repristinating "pure" biblical teaching or "New Testament church principles." I absorbed this through my conversion amongst the Plymouth

Brethren, but the same primitivism characterized the Pentecostal churches of which you and I were a part. It's the leapfrogging I've suggested before: leaping over the gifts of teachers like Augustine and Ambrose, as if we are somehow better equipped to read the Scriptures on our own. In a strange way, such hubris reflects the chronological snobbery of the Enlightenment, which saw liberation from tradition as the mark of "rational" maturity. Paradoxically, this is why such primitivism is actually quite *modern*.

In contrast to this, the Reformers are "catholic" because they are *incarnational*. They take seriously Jesus's promise that the Spirit will guide us into all truth (John 16:13). This is an extension of God's "accommodation" to us in the incarnation of the Son. It is above all to affirm that the church is indeed Christ's body, animated by the Spirit. This means that the Spirit is living and active in Christ's body *in* and *across* time. So while Calvin might have lamented what he saw, in Luther's terms, as the "Babylonian captivity of the church," he nonetheless also conceded that the church persisted in (and in spite of) the church of Rome.

So if I (admittedly provocatively) tease you that "to be Reformed is to be catholic," in all seriousness I don't mean to be a tease. It's just that sometimes I worry that your Calvinist friends are trying to "out-Calvinist" John Calvin! I'm hoping you'll see the catholicity of the Reformed tradition as an outgrowth of the central affirmation of the incarnation: God's breaking into time for our sakes.

Well, this letter's become a bit of a deluge, now that I look at it. Apologies for my verbosity.

With all best wishes,

On Being "Confessional"

Dear Jesse,

Great question—and one that directly flows out of what we've been talking about recently. Your asking the question encourages me that you're absorbing the "logic" of my previous letter. So let me take a shot at answering it.

When a church or tradition describes itself as "confessional," as many of the Reformed churches do, it means that it sees creeds and confessions as formulations of the "doctrinal standards" for the church, as trusted guides for understanding Scripture, and as the articulated wisdom for shaping discipleship. Maybe it would help if we considered some specifics and got some names on the table.

First, note the distinction between creeds and confessions. "Creeds" usually refers to the historic documents of the church, forged in the first centuries of the church fathers. These were the fruit of ecumenical councils that brought together a wide array of the church, so they are sometimes described as the "ecumenical creeds." They are also statements that were forged before the first great schism of the church—the break between East and West (giving us, roughly, Eastern Orthodoxy and "Roman" Catholicism). These earliest creeds are affirmed by all Christians, because they are the oldest memory of the church, you might say. So when we're talking about creeds, we're referring to the Apostles' Creed—the most succinct summary of Christian faith, which arose as a baptismal formula for confessing the faith upon baptism—and the fuller statements of faith we find in the Nicene Creed and the Athanasian Creed, which are robust, nuanced articulations of trinitarian faith.

"Confessions," on the other hand, refers to later documents and statements of faith that assume and build on these earlier creeds. Often catechisms are understood to be part and parcel of these confessions. These are usually statements that arose during and out of the Reformation, especially in the sixteenth and seventeenth centuries. I often think of these in terms of "continental" confessions that were forged on the continent in Europe, and "Anglo" confessions that were the products of English and Scottish Reformations. So the continental confessions would include the Lutheran Augsburg Confession, but also more specifically Calvinist standards such as the Belgic Confession, the Heidelberg Catechism, and the Canons of Dort. Anglo confessions would include the Thirty-Nine Articles and the Westminster Confession of Faith, along with Westminster's Larger and Shorter Catechisms. Reformed churches are generally subject to what I'm calling continental confessions, while Presbyterian churches generally adopt Anglo standards, and the Westminster Confession in particular.

Now *none* of the traditions or denominations that describe themselves as "confessional" would ever see the creeds or confessions as on a par with Scripture, nor would they ever claim they are infallible. The confessions, and even the creeds, are subject to the authority of Scripture—which is alone infallible. The creeds and confessions *serve* Scripture. You might think of them in a few different ways. For example, the Heidelberg Catechism itself describes the Apostles' Creed as a "summary" of the gospel. So here you have this interesting layering: the Heidelberg Catechism is itself a later "confession." And a significant chunk of the catechism's summary and explanation of the Christian faith (in qq. 23–58) is an explanation of the creed. But the catechism sees the creed as already a crystallization of faith more fully articulated in the Scriptures. So according to the catechism, the "gospel is summarized for us in the articles of our Christian faith—a creed beyond doubt and confessed throughout the world" (q. 22).

Or a second example: you might think of the creeds and confessions as a kind of *plot summary*. Not exactly "CliffsNotes," but rather a summation and overview. The point isn't to *replace* the story but to provide a portal *into* the bigger story. Keep in mind that the catechisms in particular were often written to help young people grow into the faith, so there's a pedagogical function here.

Or finally, you might think of the creeds and confessions as articulating the *grammar* of the language of faith. They're not meant to be a substitute for speaking the language! Rather, they provide a way for one to learn a "second" language. If I'm studying Greek grammar, it's not so that I can know Greek grammar; it's so that I can *read Greek*, and perhaps the Greek New Testament in particular. So also, I learn the "grammar" of faith articulated in the creeds and confessions, not as ends in themselves, but as an invitation to read Scripture well, and as guides for faithful practice.

"Confessional" churches in the Reformed tradition nonetheless receive the creeds and confessions as gifts. If, as Scripture promises, the ascended Lord gives to the church the gifts of apostles, prophets, teachers, and pastors in order to "prepare God's people for works of service, so that the body of Christ may be built up until we all reach unity in the faith and in the knowledge of the

Son of God and become mature, attaining to the whole measure of the fullness of Christ" (Eph. 4:12–13); and if he gives such gifts so that we are not blown about by every wind of doctrine (v. 14); then you could say that the Reformed tradition sees the creeds and confessions as gifts from these gifts. That is, the creeds and confessions are the fruit of the Spirit-led wisdom of teachers across the ages of the church, which are "handed down" (*traditio*) to us as gifts.

I hope you can see how this grows out of the sensibility we discussed in the last letter: there is a fundamental affirmation of the history of the church at work here, which is based on trust in the Spirit's promise to lead us into all truth. In fact, maybe we should instead say that the Reformed tradition is a "creedal" or "confessional" tradition because of a fundamental trust that the Spirit of Christ is at work in history in an *incarnational* way—that the church *is* Christ's body, as he promised; and that he has not left us to our own devices, nor has he left us orphans, but he has given his Spirit of power and illumination, and that Spirit is living and active in Christ's body, which is *us*, the church. Indeed, if we followed up on this, we might suggest that those sectors of Christendom that are "anti-creedal" are actually kind of gnostic in their suspicion of history. Just like various heresies that denied the humanity of Christ, I think those who don't embrace the legacy of orthodox creeds and confessions are, in a way, rejecting Christ's body *again*.

Ultimately, such "Bible-only," anti-creedal traditions (those traditions that reject "tradition"!) are spurning the gifts promised us by Christ through his Spirit.

Gosh, I'm sorry! This letter has become interminable! I hope you'll take my long-windedness as itself a testimony of how much I value the *gifts* of the creeds and confessions. I have much more to share with you about this, but I'll dam the deluge for now.

In Christ,

P.S. I sent you that little gray book, *Ecumenical Creeds and Reformed Confessions*, a while back, right? I hope this might encourage you to dig that up. When you next have a chance, read the Heidelberg Catechism in one sitting.

P.P.S. Sorry, I left this letter sitting overnight and now just have to add something while I'm thinking of it. I first encountered Reformed confessions in the Westminster Catechism, and then the Westminster Confession of Faith. It was probably reading Piper that turned me on to the catechism with that wonderful opening line: "What is the chief end of man? To glorify God and enjoy him forever" (which, as you know, Piper glosses—in good

Augustinian fashion—as "To glorify God *by* enjoying him forever"). Anyway, I found the Westminster standards illuminating and challenging.

But I have to confess that when I discovered the Heidelberg Catechism, it was like discovering a nourishing oasis compared to the arid desert of Westminster's cool scholasticism. The God of the Heidelberg Catechism is not just a Sovereign Lord of the Universe, nor merely the impartial Judge at the trial of justification; the God of the Heidelberg Catechism keeps showing up as a *Father*. For example, when expounding the first article of the Apostles' Creed ("I believe in God, the Father almighty, creator of heaven and earth"), the Heidelberg Catechism discusses all the ways that God upholds the universe by his hand, but also affirms that this sovereign Creator attends to me, a speck in that universe. And it concludes the answer to question 26 by summarizing: "He is able to do this because he is almighty God; he desires to do this because he is a faithful Father."

Could Reformed theology perhaps speak not only to our intellectual passions and theological curiosity, but also our deepest fears and needs? You know what I'm talking about, Jesse. It hasn't been easy for either of us as we've tried to make our way in the world without fathers. But whenever I read this question in the catechism, I'm reminded (and overwhelmed) that through Christ I have found a "faithful" Father who will never leave me. Or rather, that Father has found me—has chased me down and called me to himself.

Do you, like me, ever wonder if your absent (earthly) father is thinking about you? Do you spend some nights secretly wondering if your father might someday call you? More often than I can tell, I secretly long to get that most awkward phone call in the world, which would just confirm that my father remembers I exist. Why do I want that so much?

But while some days it's small comfort, it *is* nonetheless comfort to be reminded that I do have a "faithful Father" who not only knows I exist, but also came and found me.

I think this is also why the benediction at the conclusion of worship is something I crave. It's that moment when my "faithful Father" says to me what I wish and wish and wish I'd hear from my absent, earthly father. In fact, at the risk of looking the fool, I'm including here a poem (or a sorry excuse for a poem) I once scribbled in my notebook.

Benediction

I've been waiting all week for this:
The minister's arms raised in awkward
    sanctity—
a peculiar bend at his shoulders and elbows
that make me think he can't throw a baseball
and was probably beat up a lot on the
    playground.

But now his soft hands with slender fingers,
nervously trembling above shoulders quickly
    tired,
have become conduits of blessing.

And we are there waiting,
hands hungrily outstretched,
greedy for any scrap of grace we might receive
from this ersatz Father,
panting for benediction.

Beyond Westminster

Dear Jesse,

I'm sorry. I didn't mean to get all "mushy" in that last (long!) letter. (And please burn that poem immediately. ☺) But I appreciate your reply and am grateful for your prayers. My hope is that you'll get a sense that Calvinism is not primarily a theological "system"; it is a *spirituality*—a "piety," as the Puritans would have said (this is what I most remember from J. I. Packer's wonderful book *A Quest for Godliness: The Puritan Vision of the Christian Life*). The Reformed tradition isn't an intellectual framework to make us "smart" Christians (enabling us to then look down on other "dumb" Christians). It isn't a theological complex to be admired for its coherence and theoretical beauty. It is first and foremost an articulation of Jesus's call to discipleship. Calvinism isn't worth a thing—it will be merely a clanging cymbal—if it doesn't engender a way of life that exhibits the gracious compassion of God lived out in a people who are a foretaste of his coming kingdom.

I don't want anything to do with a Calvinism that doesn't answer the first question of the Heidelberg Catechism: "What is my only *comfort* in life and in death?" I'm not saying that we need theological frameworks that coddle us and whisper sweet nothings in our ear. But I am saying that Calvinism isn't worth a lick if it doesn't translate into a set of practices that mark us as a peculiar people who are adopted brothers and sisters of the Beloved (Col. 1:13).

As I said, I *feel* that difference between the Westminster Confession and Catechisms and the Heidelberg Catechism and Belgic Confession. The latter ("continental") confessions have an existential *esprit* about them that seems to seep into my soul in a way that Westminster's more "logical" approach does not.

Actually, there's another difference between these I'd like to note—not in order to bash the Westminster divines, but in order to try to get at something I've noted earlier about the catholicity of the Reformed tradition. As soon as you have a chance, read through the Heidelberg Catechism (if you didn't heed my exhortation last time!), and then read through, say, the Westminster Shorter Catechism. And tell me whether you don't, like me, feel a difference. I don't mean to go all "Oprah" here; I just mean, read them side by side and I think you'll sense and see a difference between them. What is it?

I suggest it's this: the Heidelberg Catechism articulates the gospel that must be believed *by* articulating the Apostles' Creed, whereas the Creed doesn't even make a showing in the Westminster Shorter Catechism. (I think some editions "annex" the creed to the catechism, but it's not inscribed in the heart of the catechism.) Why does that make a difference? Well, I think it goes to something we've been talking about for a while now: by inscribing the Creed right into the heart of the catechism—by relying on the Apostles' Creed as a succinct, faithful "summary" of the Gospel—the Heidelberg Catechism receives the tradition as a gift, and thereby situates itself *in* the church catholic (as, of course, the Creed itself does when we confess our belief in "the holy, catholic church"). This is to see ourselves as heirs of a tradition, indebted to the communion of the saints, and thus as part of a body that is much older than us, and much bigger than us (confessed "throughout the world"). That, I think, is an important sensibility that is notably absent in the Westminster standards.

And I think it matters because it explains something I've hinted at before. Let me try to articulate this in a way that I hope isn't too polemical. Be patient with me as I try to work this out.

Let's put it this way: the "Calvinist" radio program you're listening to, the books you're reading, and the crew of "young Calvinists" you're hanging out with are, let's say, "Westminster" Calvinists. Not that there's anything wrong with that! ☺ But I only mean to say that this is a stream of the Reformed tradition with particular emphases and "pet" concerns. It is one particular articulation of the Reformed understanding of the gospel. And I'm suggesting that there might be something important missing from this stream, something that was, in fact, central for Luther and Calvin (not to mention Augustine)—namely, an emphasis on *the church*. Or, to put it in terms we've been discussing: this Westminster stream diminishes the *catholicity* of the Reformed tradition, so the "Calvinism" that it articulates is just the sort of slimmed-down, extracted soteriology that can be basically detached and then inserted across an array of denominations (and "non-denominations"). And so you get that strange phenomenon I've noted before: that a place like Southern Baptist Theological Seminary could be a vibrant center of Calvinism.

Now, if by "Calvinism" we only meant a TULIP-shaped soteriology focused on the salvation of individuals' souls ("the elect"), then I grant that there's nothing inherently strange about Baptists adopting that specific soteriological stance. Indeed, it's not even surprising, since I think it is the best, most coherent way to read the (admittedly scandalous) picture we see painted in Scripture. But the Reformed tradition is not just a soteriology, because the Reformation was not just about a doctrine of salvation. Take Calvin as an example: for him, the Reformation was not just about reforming the doctrine of personal salvation; it was also about the reform of the church as a body and an institution. And in this respect, he was concerned with reforming the church's worship precisely because he thought discipleship was at stake. So Calvin and the Reformers had significant concerns about the *structure* of the church and the relationship between congregations. He couldn't have imagined the sorts of "autonomous" congregations we see in Baptist and non-denominational churches. Indeed, by the end of his life, as a result of his pastoral concern for the life of the faithful in Geneva, Calvin actually affirmed something like an episcopal structure of bishops (as articulated in the 1543 edition of his *Institutes*). But at the very least, one of the outcomes of the Reformation was a church polity (i.e., organization of the church) that the Reformer saw flowing from the emphases of the Reformation. So *church matters* for the Reformed tradition; or more specifically, *how* we "do" church matters. How we *worship* matters.

Even more than that, Calvin thought the implications of the gospel spilled beyond not only the individual, but also the church, into the reformation of society. If the Lord is the Lord of all, then Christ's lordship reigns over "all things" (Col. 1:15–20). Interestingly, for Calvin this did *not* translate into a penchant for theocracy. In fact, his reforms in Geneva were significant for shaping the later history of democracy (as shown in John Witte Jr.'s recent book *The Reformation of Rights*). But we'll have to discuss that another time.

All I mean to emphasize is this: the Reformed tradition is about much more than TULIP because it's about much more than the individual. The Reformed tradition is not just a soteriology; it also issues in an ecclesiology, a doctrine of the church—and not just a doctrine of the church, but renewed ecclesial practice centered in worship. The Reformers were fundamentally concerned about the shape of the church as the body of Christ—both as the site where the gospel is proclaimed and as the place where disciples are sanctified. They didn't think the church's worship was a matter of taste or preference, nor did they think the organization of the church was a matter of human ingenuity. And this is why they couldn't have imagined the fruit of the "doctrines of grace" being unhooked from the ecclesial soil of Reformed worship and church polity. Rather, the Reformers saw a "logic" to worship that grows organically out of their understanding of sin and redemption.

So how did a Baptist seminary become a hotbed of "Calvinism"? Well (and don't broadcast this to your friends right away), I'm suggesting that, perhaps in a way, the "Westminster-ization" of the Reformed tradition squeezed out this wider picture of the Reformed tradition—a picture that is preserved in what I've called the "continental" confessions. And because it was the Westminster version of the Reformed tradition (or "Calvinism") that has been the most popular version in the United States, you could then see how Baptists and non-denominational churches (which all tend to be anti-creedal and anti-sacramental) thought they could absorb Calvinism without it affecting the shape of their worship or polity.

I don't mean to be snobby about this. It's just that, in my own pilgrimage to the Reformed tradition, while it might have been the soteriology that initially hooked my interest, it has been the *wider* aspects of the Reformed tradition (its ecclesiology and its engagement with culture) that have sustained my devotion. It's as if God baited me with election, but when I was hooked, he pulled me into the church.

All best,

LETTER XIII

God's "Social" Gospel

Dear Jesse,

No, I'm not saying that God isn't concerned about individuals, or that the Reformed tradition discounts "personal salvation." Not at all. To say that God is concerned with *more* than the salvation of individual souls is *not* to say that he's interested in *less* than the salvation of individuals. For example, if I said football is about more than just running and passing—that it's also about character and virtue and discipline—would you conclude that therefore football is *not* about running and passing? (Admittedly, given that you're a Carolina Panthers fan, this illustration might be lost on you—since they can't really run or pass. Watch the Eagles for a change and this example might sink in! ☺)

Maybe I could put it this way: the Reformed tradition emphasizes that, from the beginning, the "basic unit" of God's dealing with humanity is not individuals but a *people*. God—who, as Trinity of Father, Son, and Spirit, is already a kind of community of love—doesn't create the world in order to produce a collection of solitary individuals or social "atoms" that are self-enclosed, utterly distinct, and thus "privately" related to God in vertical silos. Right from creation, God creates a *people*, reflected in the two-ness of creation when God creates humanity in the couple of Adam and Eve.

I think there is an entire theology packed into the pronouns of Scripture. (The Puritans used to emphasize that "God loveth adverbs." I think he also cares about pronouns.) From that opening "us" of the creational word in Genesis 1:26 ("Let us make man in our image"), to the "them" of Genesis 1:27 ("male and female he created them"), to the plural "you" of the creational mandate in Genesis 1:29 ("I give you every seed-bearing plant"), God's creation is laden with plurals! (It's also a little tough to be "fruitful and multiply" all by yourself, if you know what I mean.) The abundance of God's creative love yields the creation of a community, not a collection of individuals—which is also why the "them" of Adam and Eve mirrors and images their social Creator when they become "fruitful and multiply." The overflowing of their love in the creation of a family is an echo of God's own creation. God is not some cosmic hermit or introvert; nor does he create individual humans in order for them to just have a private, "personal relationship with Jesus." Of course a people "includes" individuals, and God knows the number of hairs on our head. I don't mean to deny that the Creator of the universe is—unbelievably!—intimately concerned with *me*, loves *me*. But God's interest in his creatures is more than just the sum of the individual parts. God creates a *people*.

God also *saves* a people. God's election echoes his creation. Just as he created a people, so he calls a people. When God's electing call comes to Abraham, it is not just to Abraham. It's to Abraham and his people, and this call will set a whole motley crew traipsing across that Middle Eastern desert toward Canaan. The "unit" of God's dealing, I'm suggesting, is always a community, a people. And of course God elects Abraham precisely in order to (re)create a people who can be God's image-bearers—a "great nation" that will be a blessing to the world (Gen. 12:1–5). This communal dealing of God starts to get pretty tangible in Genesis 17: When God declares that the mark of his covenant with Abraham will be circumcision (Gen. 17:9–14), all the males in the "household" received this mark of promise (Gen. 17:23). You don't hear them saying, "Well, God made the covenant with Abraham, not me, so thanks, but I'll pass." (And they certainly had good motivation to do so.) The "you" of God's dealings is always an "us." The gospel is always already a *social* gospel.

The "plural" nature of God's dealings with humanity—God's *people*-centric economy of salvation (rather than a *person*-centric picture)—continues to replay itself throughout Scripture in the calling of Israel and ultimately in the calling out of the *ekklesia*, the church, the people of God. Think of all those "you's" in the New Testament! Our location in individualist America makes us tend to read those "you's" as if the Bible was privately addressed to *me*—as if the "you" was singular. But the "you" is almost always plural. The "you" is *us*. It's not *me*, but *we*. So it's not primarily that I am a chosen individual. Instead, the gospel announces that *we* are a chosen *people*. This is stunningly captured in Peter's announcement that brings to mind God's earlier dealings with his people: "But you are a chosen people, a royal priesthood, a holy nation, a people belonging to God, that you may declare the praises of him who called you out of darkness into his wonderful light. Once you were not a people, but now you are the people of God; once you had not received mercy, but now you have received mercy" (1 Pet. 2:9–10). Can you hear the plurality and community and *people*-ness laden in that "you"? God is not only interested in soul-saving; God is interested in "nation-building," calling and re-creating a people, making a people out of individuals who were *not* otherwise a "people." God is only in the soul-saving business because he's in the people-building business.

Thanks be to God,

P.S. When you start reading Scripture in this light, all of a sudden you see things you hadn't noticed before. For instance, at times Paul seems to suggest that in Christ, God has constituted a new "race" that transcends the distinction between Jew and Gentile. For instance, writing to the Christians in Corinth, he'll remind them of a time when they *were* Gentiles (1 Cor. 12:2). In a similar way, in Galatians Paul emphasizes how the gospel undercuts any ethnic claim to being a member of God's people (Gal. 3:26–29). It's as if God is constituting a kind of "third race," a new people.

Unfortunately, the Reformed tradition—though it rightly emphasizes this people-centric view of God's relationship to creation—has also fallen into traps that have failed to appreciate the radical implications of this. Indeed, there were renditions of Reformed theology in both the American South and South Africa that were very bent on maintaining heinously unjust distinctions *between Gentiles*, that is, between blacks and whites. This is why a Reformed confession like the Belhar Confession is so significant in naming the sins of the Reformed tradition in this respect. I encourage you to take a look at it; it's readily available on the web.

Our Promise-Keeping God

Dear Jesse,

You caught me! I was trying to sort of work on the sly, fly under the radar, covertly inviting you into an idea without yet naming it. But you're right: that "people-centric" picture I sketched last time was trying to get at what I take to be the heart of the Reformed tradition's emphasis in the Scriptural leitmotif of *covenant*. In short, the last letter was meant to be a mini-introduction to covenant theology. So you've heard of this already, then?

I'm glad to hear it, since I must confess that I'm often a bit perplexed—or at least puzzled—by all the folks I hear calling themselves "Calvinists" or "Reformed" who talk about the Rapture and basically buy into a Left

Behind–style eschatology (or doctrine of "last things"). That Left Behind ecclesiology grows out of soil that is decidedly un-Reformed, in no small part because it buys into the Jesus-and-me picture of individual salvation we were talking about. In other words, it fails to see that since creation, and even in spite of the fall, God has been creating and calling *one* "people" to be his own.

This understanding of God's covenantal faithfulness isn't primarily about the future or concerned with the "end times." So, though I've already hinted that covenant theology stands in contrast to dispensationalism, I'd rather not be distracted by end-times scenarios here (for relevant discussion of these sorts of concerns, see Vern Poythress's little book *Understanding Dispensationalists*). What's most significant about covenant theology is not how it thinks about "the Rapture" (it doesn't!) or the millennium, but how it shapes our understanding of the *present*—more specifically, how it makes sense of God's faithfulness across the entire narrative of Scripture, and how it primes us to appreciate the people-centric nature of God's creative and redemptive action.

Others have laid out the basics of Reformed covenant theology much better than I could (I think I already mentioned Michael Horton's book *Introducing Covenant Theology*). I would just highlight what we already broached last time: the merciful grace of God condescends to save a *people*, and thus God binds himself to an "us." God makes a promise and calls us to respond to that promise. But, grace upon grace, God keeps his promise even when we don't! When through the covenants (with Adam and Eve, with Noah, with Abraham, with Israel) we show ourselves continually unable to keep up our end of the bargain, prone to wandering eyes and hearts like Gomer (Hosea 1:2–2:1), God finally makes a promise that ends all promises: he promises not only to stipulate the conditions of the covenant but also to provide the *power* to keep the covenant (Jer. 31). And it is the reality of that new covenant that is marked at the Last Supper, where God-in-the-flesh sits down with wretches like us to seal the deal. And then we realize he's taking all the burdens of the covenant on himself, including all our inabilities and refusals to keep it. The cup that is the covenant "in His blood" anticipates and reminds us that the covenant comes to its climax in the God-man who, as God, articulates the conditions of the covenant and, as human (the second Adam), is finally the first human being to faithfully keep the promise (Luke 22:20). And the risen, covenant-keeping Son of God bequeaths to us his Spirit, both to seal us as members of this covenant people and to empower us to keep the covenant (Rom. 8:1–5).

What I find most compelling about this picture is that it helps us see the Scriptures as one narrative, one unfolding drama in multiple acts or chapters, rather than seeing it as either a series of private dealings between God and individuals or a chopped-up conglomeration of discrete epochs or dispensations in which God seems to keep changing the rules. The basic lineaments of the narrative are simple and unchanging: the Creator of the universe establishes norms and standards for his creatures ("the law") and requires them to obey. In the face of their original disobedience, he doesn't suspend those norms or standards; rather, he keeps calling humanity to that standard while at the same time graciously enacting countermeasures. But the call is the same: humanity, created in God's image, is called to bear his image as Yahweh's ambassadors, his vice-regents in the territory of creation, by continuing to unfold and unpack all the potential that has been folded into creation. And he calls us to do that *well*, in ways that accord with his norms and desire for the final flourishing of his creation "to the praise of his glorious grace" (Eph. 1:6). The core of the covenant remains the same. Unfortunately, our covenantal infidelity also remains constant—until the climax of the covenant when a Son of Mary lives up to the calling on our behalf, and then makes it possible for us, by grace, to live up to the covenant.

By helping us see that God has always been creating and calling a people "that are his very own" (Titus 2:14), covenant theology emphasizes a *continuity* to the people of God. Thus you'll hear the Reformers and Puritans talk about "the church" in the Old Testament—which is just a shorthand, anachronistic way to emphasize that God's called-out people, his *ek-klesia*, constitutes one people across time. Why is that important? Well, consider just one reason: reading the Scriptures in this way makes the Old Testament come to life again! This is why preaching the Old Testament is a significant part of Reformed worship. And as I've been trying to emphasize, the Reformers saw worship as central to discipleship.

Well, I fear I've rambled a little. My hope is that you'll see this notion of "covenant" as another aspect of the wider Reformed tradition and appreciate how it reconfigures our understanding of Christian faith. It's a theme that bubbles up from the Scriptures themselves, and once we appreciate that, it also helps us see the same Scripture with new eyes. Above all, it helps us understand the gracious condescension of our promise-keeping Lord.

Gratefully,

Jesse

4955 El Segundo Blvd.

Hawthorne, CA 90250

Postcard from Amsterdam

Jesse,

Sorry I've been out of touch. This postcard will explain why: I've been here in Amsterdam for a seminar on theology and politics, hosted by the university founded by Abraham Kuyper, the Free University of Amsterdam. I think the first time I ever heard of the Free University was in R. C. Sproul's novel *Thy Brother's Keeper*. (Yes, you read that right: a *novel* by R. C. Sproul! Actually, it's probably a bit scary how much I learned from Sproul's one venture into fiction.) Anyway, it's fun being here in this school of Dutch Reformed lore—though it's no longer the school that Kuyper dreamed up in the late nineteenth century. Still, what sort of Calvinism makes one found, not a seminary, but a university?

More later,

Elected to Love

Dear Jesse,

I can completely sympathize with your conundrum. And I figured this issue would arise soon enough. I can imagine how your study along these lines has made you increasingly uncomfortable in your current "church home," as you put it. I remember my own struggles with these issues. Indeed, I *still* struggle with them.

Before getting at some of the issues, would you permit me to offer a preemptive caution and exhortation? These are serious matters. And no matter how you might currently think of your congregation's "doctrine," I want you to remember what I know and witnessed: that they have been the hands and feet of Jesus to you. While they might not be "teaching" what you want to hear (and what you think is important), they have been *living* the gracious compassion of a sovereign Lord. They welcomed you off the streets of Inglewood, with all your warts and baggage, all your brokenness hidden in that gang-trained swagger, and they showed you the love of a faithful, compassionate Father. They introduced you to Jesus, and Jesus met you in their embraces. The congregation you've called home these last years was God's conduit for your "effectual calling." While you are now increasingly interested in theology and doctrine, don't forget that you were *loved* into the kingdom of God. And such love is closer to the heart of our gracious, electing God than any cool, intellectual grasp of the details of predestination.

So, before you start congratulating yourself on your understanding of the doctrines of grace (I'm talking to my younger self here!), and before you start looking down on your sisters and brothers at church, please remember that they have loved you into this place—that you have matured in the faith to the point of contemplating these matters only because the church has buoyed you with compassion and hospitality. (Remember: not only Calvinists are elect! Thanks be to God, understanding the doctrines of election and predestination is not a condition for being elect.)

I apologize if I'm criticizing you for a sort of phantom failure. As I said, I'm really speaking to my younger self, and this exhortation is my way of saying I wish

I'd done some things differently. So please receive it in the spirit in which it's intended. I love you, and I know the folks at your church there do, too. I don't want you to lose sight of that.

  Peace,

Church Matters

Dear Jesse,

Sorry! You're right: I didn't really answer your question. With my caution from last time as a context (and thanks for receiving that in the spirit in which it was meant), let's then consider the issue. Fortunately, I think our recent discussions about covenant are a helpful way to frame what's at stake in considering a church home.

First, despite the way you frame the question, I *don't* think you should approach this as a matter of finding a church "that teaches Calvinism"—not because you should want to attend a church that teaches Arminianism, but because we shouldn't be thinking about church primarily in terms of teaching. The church isn't a lecture hall, and I worry that your focus on teaching actually reflects a narrow understanding of "church" that runs counter to the heart and soul of the Reformed tradition. Let me try to explain.

There's a part of our background—and part of the ethos of American evangelicalism—that we need to recognize as we're working through these issues. On the one hand, you and I were formed in a stream of the evangelical and charismatic tradition that tended to reduce "worship" to *music*. So in that approach, worship ends when the song-service ends—and then we move on to the sermon, in which we receive "teaching." I think something like this basic picture is still assumed in a lot of Baptist and non-denominational churches that consider themselves Calvinist, or perhaps even Reformed. On the other hand, evangelical folks who become interested in Reformed theology tend to fixate on the ideas and doctrines of Calvinism, and thus have a tendency to turn church into a lecture hall for arcane expositions of the fine points about election. But that's also a misunderstanding of the nature of worship.

In the Reformed tradition, the entire service is worship. While psalm singing and hymn singing might be an important part of worship, in fact they are just a slice of the entire drama that constitutes a service of Christian worship. And while the sermon is important, it too is only a part of the drama of worship. There is a specific "logic" to the entire shape of worship that flows out of the conviction that Christian worship replays the drama of the covenant. In fact, Michael Horton, in *A*

Better Way, has very helpfully described the service of Christian worship as a "covenant renewal ceremony." Worship is the site of God's action, where we dialogically encounter our Redeemer and covenantal Lord, in offers of praise and thanksgiving—but also in confession and reverence. Each week, worship invites us into the narrative of God's redemptive history. Indeed, the entire drama of worship *replays* that story each week and invites us to situate ourselves in that story. I love how Horton puts this in his big book *Covenant and Eschatology: The Divine Drama*: " 'Covenant'—and not the idea in general, but the specific praxis developed throughout redemptive history—is the culture of the people of God. . . . This redemptive-historical drama incorporates believers in such a manner that it constitutes its own cultic 'culture' " (13). Worship is our acculturation into God's people; it's where we learn to speak the language of the coming kingdom.

Let me highlight just one example of this, from one of my favorite moments in a service. In Reformed worship, when a family brings forward a child for baptism, this is not in order to superstitiously secure the child's salvation; rather, it is saying something about what we've emphasized before, which is that in the economy of God's salvation every "you" is plural, and God works with *a people*. Baptism then marks the child as a child of the covenant. In the scandalous particularity of God's electing grace, being born into a covenant family is its own grace. And the fact that the parents are bringing the child for baptism is a first sign of that grace and a recognition of our utter need for God's help. So the parents promise to "complete" this baptism, you might say, by raising the child in the faith and as part of the covenant community. But my favorite part happens at the end of the service of baptism, when the entire congregation stands. The minister then poses a question to us: "Do you, the people of the Lord, promise to receive these children in love, pray for them, help instruct them in the faith, and encourage and sustain them in the fellowship of believers?" To which we, as a people, answer: "We do, God helping us." The rituals of Reformed worship very tangibly remind us that the mundane and monumental task of raising children is *not* something we can do on our own. It takes "the village" of God's peculiar people. And even then we recognize that we can only help insofar as God helps us. So this ritual in worship both says and does a lot.

This is why the Reformed tradition has always emphasized that worship is a matter of both Word *and* sacrament. Worship is not just an opportunity to get "information" in the Word preached; it is also a ceremony in which we (re)enact the covenant with our promise-keeping God. *All* aspects of Reformed worship—the call to worship and greeting, confession and assurance of pardon, the announcement of the Law and the communal confession of the creed, the pastoral prayer for the church and the world, the preaching of the Word, the celebration of the Lord's

Supper, even the offering, sending, and benediction—*all* of these elements of worship picture what we, as "a people," are called to be. In this sense, worship is not only what is rightly owed to God; it is also a kind of *training*, a means of discipline and formation that God provides for our sanctification. Worship not only expresses our praise and adoration of God; it also forms our habits and desires. Rightly ordered worship is a crucial part of our discipleship and sanctification.

So worship isn't just a matter of "picturing" the faith or "illustrating" the story of God's redemptive action. Something also *happens* in worship. After all, the Spirit is there! There's work that gets done in worship. For example, the Heidelberg Catechism emphasizes that the Lord's Supper is not just a "sign"—not a "spectacle" to be observed as a kind of spectator sport. Rather, the Supper is also a means of nourishment and sustenance. The catechism puts it this way:

> As surely as
> I receive from the hand of the one who serves,
> and taste with my mouth
> the bread and cup of the Lord,
> given me as sure signs of Christ's body and
> blood,
> so surely
> he *nourishes* and *refreshes* my soul for eternal life
> with his crucified body and poured-out blood.
> (q. 75)

Who would want to miss out on such an opportunity to be nourished and refreshed? This is why folks like Michael Horton and Keith Mathison have recently argued, *like Calvin*, that the Lord's Supper should be a weekly part of Christian worship, woven into the fabric of every worship gathering. I agree.

So it's these sorts of concerns that you should bring when you're considering a church home. The primary mode of evaluation and discernment should not be ticking off the number of times you hear about election and predestination from the pulpit, or how often the pastor quotes Jonathan Edwards, because the fact is that a congregation could "score high" on those registers and yet still not be engaged in *worship* that is truly *Reformed*.

Let me close with one more caution: I'm not actually counseling you to leave your congregation. That is serious business and not something to be taken lightly. While I have had to wrestle through these same issues about an ecclesiastical home, I only arrived at that decision after some serious wrangling with the Spirit. Don't rush into anything.

In Christ,

P.S. In chapter 9 of *A Better Way*, Michael Horton provides a helpful answer to the question, "What should our service look like?" There he discusses the fundamental "elements" of Reformed worship. You might also remember that I unpack the core elements of worship in chapter 5 of *Desiring the Kingdom*. As I've said, I think all of these elements of worship are crucial, and as you're evaluating worship in your congregation, you'll want to be looking to see if these elements are present.

Too Reformed for Church?

Dear Jesse,

That's a common enough temptation, Jess. I understand it. I've been there. But step back and think about what you're saying: it's as if you're saying you're "too Reformed" for *any* church! How un-Reformed is that?! It seems to me that the Reformed tradition makes us all the more aware of our own personal faults and shortcomings—the myriad ways we fall short of God's holiness—as well as our utter dependence on the unmerited grace of God. How odd would it be to conclude, then, in the name of being "Reformed," that no church is "good enough" for us? In the name of Calvinism, you end up spurning the gritty particularity of what John Calvin cared about the most: *the church*—and not the church as some abstract, ethereal, pure ideal, but the church *in Geneva*, the congregations he knew and loved.

It's not about purity. (If it were, no church would ever let us in the door.) It's about faithfulness. I'm not saying that the church doesn't deserve critique. I'm just saying that recognition of the ways in which the church fails to measure up is not an excuse for being antichurch, carving out some sort of private spirituality in the name of being Reformed.

A tad grumpily,

Jesse
4955 El Segundo Blvd.
Hawthorne, CA 90250

Postcard from Seoul

Jesse,

I'll bet this is your first-ever piece of mail from Korea! But I thought this note from the Presbyterian seminary in Seoul might encourage you to realize that the Reformed tradition is not the possession of white European men. But you already knew that. (I have to admit: I don't bump into too many Mexican Calvinists! ☺) Being here in Asia reminds us that, while we might imagine the "center" of the Reformed tradition revolving around Amsterdam or Philadelphia or Grand Rapids, in fact there are vibrant centers (plural!) all around God's creation—in Korea and Japan, in Brazil and Cuba, in Ghana and Indonesia. Calvinism is not an inherently European invention—even if its provenance is Geneva. Its *ultimate* provenance and source is the Creator of every corner of the globe.

With every good wish,

On Grumpy Speculations

Dear Jesse,

I had a long drive recently, during which I listened to some of the CDs you so generously sent. The experience left me with an admittedly snide question: Why does the crew of "new Calvinists" you're attracted to all seem so, well, *grumpy*?

I've been grateful that I haven't detected this same tone in you (except for a brief flash a few months ago). But I must confess that I tire a bit of the CDs you've kindly shared, largely because these men (and *there's* a question for another time) seem to spend more time bashing other Christians than they do denouncing the idolatries of our age. In fact, if these sermons and lectures are any indication, you'd think these folks see Pentecostalism as *more* of a danger to our souls than capitalism—or Willow Creek as more of a threat than the temptations of nationalism. It's like they have a myopic fixation on the "Arminian" errors of other Christians and thus miss the downright diabolical systems of injustice that are all around us. I think they'd profit from a rereading of Bunyan's *Pilgrim's Progress* and his attention to the sly temptations of "Vanity Fair." I have a hard time believing that the denial of limited atonement is the most pressing matter of discipleship right now. We should be more worried about Walmart.

I also tire of their misplaced confidence in their own theological speculations, as well as their pride in pristine systems of scholastic distinctions by which they carve up mysteries that have led giants before us to tremble. (In this connection, I couldn't stop thinking of the joke Augustine cites in the *Confessions*: "What was God doing before he made the heaven and earth? . . . Preparing hell for people who ask that sort of question!" [11.12.14].) The Scriptures are not a storehouse of propositions for system building; they are the narrative story and unfolding drama of God's redemptive action—but you'd never know that from these sermons, which, in the name of Calvinism, fail to actually submit themselves to the authority of God's Word. Instead, they're domesticating the prophetic force of that Word by cramming it into a system. I'm sorry, but I have little patience for that. Our incarnational God is both too big and too messy for such pigeonholing. In this vein, I'm reminded of a comment Augustine made to his congregation in one of his sermons:

> But you are quite unable to imagine or think of such a thing. And such ignorance is more religious and devout than any presumption of knowledge. After all, we are talking about God. It says, *and the Word was God* (Jn. 1:1). We are talking about God; so why be surprised if you cannot grasp it? I mean, if you can grasp it, it isn't God. Let us rather make a devout confession of ignorance, instead of a brash profession of knowledge. Certainly it is great bliss to have a little touch or taste of God with the mind; but to completely grasp him, to comprehend him, is altogether impossible. (Sermon 117.5)

If Calvinism is just a system that gives us pride in denouncing the supposed simplicity and ignorance of our sisters and brothers in Christ, then you can keep it. I have no interest in flying under a banner that is just a cover for haughty theological speculation at the expense of charity.

And I think John Calvin would agree. In fact, I was just reading a collection of his letters and came across this admonition he sent to a younger theologian:

> I am very greatly grieved that the fine talents with which God has endowed you, should be occupied not only with what is vain and fruitless, but that they should also be injured by pernicious figments. What I warned you of

long ago, I must again seriously repeat, that unless you correct in time this itching after investigation, it is to be feared you will bring upon yourself severe suffering. I should be cruel towards you did I treat with a show of indulgence what I believe to be a very dangerous error. I should prefer, accordingly, offending you a little at present by my severity, rather than allow you to indulge unchecked in the fascinating allurements of curiosity. The time will come, I hope, when you will rejoice in having been so violently admonished. Adieu, brother very highly esteemed by me; and if this rebuke is harsher than it ought to be, ascribe it to my love to you. (*The Letters of John Calvin*, p. 129)

How beautifully bold of Calvin to write such an exhortation. And notice Calvin's own caution about "speculation" and "curiosity." God's Word gives us quite enough to chew on without having to hungrily and greedily start flying off into the unaccountability of building "systems" where God is silent.

Yours,

P.S. OK, I can't quite resist saying a bit more about the "men" comment. My position on women in office (and marriage) is no secret to you (given our Sunday school discussions about complementarian vs. egalitarian understandings of marriage). What you might find surprising, or perhaps disconcerting, is that it was a Reformed hermeneutic that led me to that position. The narrative dynamic of Creation-Fall-Redemption is the lens through which I think about these gender-related issues. The C-F-R dynamic, you'll recall, begins with a *good* creation, is attentive to *all* the ways that the fall has cursed creation (both human and nonhuman), and understands God's redemption as the salvation of "all things" (Col. 1:20). In other words, the effect of salvation is to roll back the effects of the curse (Gen. 3); so in the words of our Christmas hymn, Christ's redemption reaches "far as the curse is found." The curse isn't just personal; it isn't just about individual sin. The curse of the fall affects all of creation (the serpent, the ground, fauna, our work); even our systems and institutions are accursed. So the good news of redemption has to reach into those spheres as well. This is why cancer research and sustainable agriculture and literacy training are all aspects of rolling back the curse.

As I read it, the subjection of women is bound up with the fall, not creation (see Gen. 3:16), which is why the announcement of the gospel impinges on this disordered aspect of creation, rolling back the effect of the curse. That takes time to become a reality, just as it took time for us to appreciate the heinous injustice of slavery. But on the other hand, Jesus's and Paul's appreciation of the importance of women was already scandalous given the cultural norms of the day. So in a way, the effect of redemption in this area only "rolled out" over time.

I don't expect this will be sufficient to convince you! But I only hope you might appreciate how someone could take this position, not as a "liberal" departure from the Reformed tradition, but actually as a concrete working-out of a Reformed understanding of Scripture and salvation.

Wide-Angle Calvinism

Dear Jesse,

What?! You've started to think that being a "Calvinist" is not necessarily synonymous with being "Reformed"? Well, then, my work here is done. ☺

But you're right, and I'm encouraged that you put it that way: "Reformed" is perhaps not reducible to "Calvinism," and not even "Calvinism" reduces down to a soteriology or a fixation on TULIP. Nor can it be captured in one doctrine such as sovereignty or election or even God's glory. Indeed, I hope you've got the sense that I wouldn't want to "boil down" Calvinism or the Reformed tradition to any *one* point or doctrine or idea. I've been trying to emphasize that the Reformation—and hence, the Reformed tradition—was a comprehensive and complex renewal movement that had implications not only for the doctrine of salvation but also for ecclesiology, for worship, for discipleship, even for cultural engagement in and for the world. Calvinism is less like a wheel protruding from one single hub and more like a garden tended by a Gardener who wants to see a thousand flowers bloom. It's less a foundational doctrine and more a comprehensive vision.

I came to appreciate this rich, comprehensive understanding of Calvinism from its Dutch stream, and from Abraham Kuyper in particular. Indeed, Kuyper's 1898 Stone Lectures at Princeton Seminary—published simply under the title *Calvinism*—should be an essential part of your library. In his opening lecture, on Calvinism as a "life-system," Kuyper cautions against reducing Calvinism to a specifically doctrinal matter, and to a specific doctrine in particular. "In this sense," he notes, "a Calvinist is represented exclusively as the outspoken subscriber to the dogma of fore-ordination" (13). But as he points out, even ardent defenders of predestination such as Charles Hodge resisted the reduction of Calvinism to this one point, and thus preferred to describe themselves as "Augustinians" (as do I). In contrast, throughout these lectures Kuyper articulates Calvinism as, variously, a "complex," a "life-system," a "general tendency," a "general system of life," and, finally, a "world- and life-view." As such, he doesn't think Calvinism's competitor is something like Arminianism, but radically different, comprehensive life-systems like Islam, Buddhism, and modernism. Every life-system, according to Kuyper, not only spells out how "I" can be saved but spells out an entire vision *of* and *for* the totality of human life, ultimately articulating an understanding of three "fundamental relations of all human life": our relation to God, our relation to other persons (and human flourishing in general), and humanity's relation to the natural world. And Calvinism, Kuyper claims, is nothing less than such a "complex," such a "life-system." Indeed, he thinks Calvinism was, in its own sense, revolutionary:

> Calvinism has wrought an entire change in the world of thoughts and conceptions. In this also, placing itself before the face of God, it has not only honored *man* for the sake of his likeness to the Divine image [thus giving rise to democracy—lecture 3], but also *the world* as a Divine creation [giving rise to modern science—lecture 4], and has at once placed to the front the great principle that there is a *particular grace* which works Salvation, and also a *common grace* by which God, maintaining the life of the world, relaxes the curse which rests upon it, arrests its process of corruption, and thus allows the untrammeled development of our life in which to glorify Himself as Creator. (29–30, Kuyper's italics)

Now, I would disagree with Kuyper on some of the specifics, but in this respect I think he's right on the money: the "genius" of Calvinism cannot be reduced to a doctrine about the salvation of elect souls. Rather, as he later emphasizes in his fourth Stone lecture, while "the Christian religion is substantially soteriological"—that is, concerned with salvation—"the object of the work of redemption is not limited to the salvation of individual sinners, but extends itself to the redemption *of the world*" (119, emphasis added), the renewal and restoration of this groaning creation (Rom. 8:18–23).

This "big-picture" sense of Calvinism—a sense that the Reformed tradition offers a complex "world- and life-view"—still owes much to the central Calvinist appreciation of sovereignty. The Calvinist emphasis on the sovereignty of a personal Creator means that the Creator has something to say about—and something to do with—every aspect of our created life. As Kuyper expressed it in another famous lecture ("Sphere Sovereignty"), at the inauguration of the Free University of Amsterdam, "There is not a single square inch of creation concerning which Christ does not say, 'Mine!'" (488). This is just another way of saying that Christ is not only Lord of our souls, but Lord of our bodies, Lord of our families, Lord of our commerce and recreation and education. He is the Lord of science and art, dance and diphthongs, eating and drinking. There's no corner of creation that is immune from his lordship, no "secular" sphere of life that is neutral with respect to the Creator's sovereignty. Calvinism, then, is about the recognition of Christ's lordship over "all things" (Col.

1:15–20). The God of Calvinism didn't just spend some precreation eternity coming up with decrees about the destination of souls. The Triune God has desires for his creation, desires for *your* flourishing, not just in your "religion," but in your work and family and play.

In his service,

P.S. Do you remember when we studied Chuck Colson's book *How Now Shall We Live?* Well, that was kind of "covert" Kuyper—Kuyper for evangelicals. We didn't hook that to "Calvinism" at the time, but I'm hoping now you might see how that comprehensive vision of the gospel impacting every sphere of life actually owes a significant debt to the Reformed tradition. You might look at it now with new eyes, and building a bridge from that to all the "new Calvinists" you've been reading might also put them in a new light.

Far as the Curse Is Found

Dear Jesse,

I don't mean to underestimate or undervalue the centrality of salvation—and the doctrine of salvation—for the Reformers. As you rightly note, when Luther nailed the Ninety-five Theses to that door in Wittenberg, he wasn't trying to start a scientific revolution or give birth to an aesthetic tradition (whether this was a *political* statement is something we'd have to discuss further). So, without question, justification was a powder-keg issue that made the Reformation explode across Europe. But in this respect, it's interesting that in his Stone lectures, Kuyper the Calvinist is critical of Luther on just this point: "Luther's starting-point was the special-soteriological principle of a justifying faith; while Calvin's [starting-point], extending far wider, lay in the general cosmological principle of the sovereignty of God" (22). Or as he later puts it in his third lecture on "Calvinism and Politics," the "dominating principle" of Calvinism "was not, soteriologically, justification by faith, but, in the widest sense cosmologically, *the Sovereignty of the Triune God over the whole Cosmos*, in all spheres and kingdoms, visible and invisible" (79, Kuyper's italics). You can see this in the very structure of the *Institutes* themselves, which begin by exploring the knowledge of God as Creator (book 1), and then our knowledge of God as Redeemer in Christ (book 2). Indeed, I wonder how many people who describe themselves as "Calvinists" today are actually more "Lutheran."

As I noted in my last letter, it's not that God isn't concerned with salvation and redemption. It's that the *scope* of God's redemptive work is bigger and wider than the rescue of individual souls. Christ's redemption is *cosmic*—it effects not only the redemption of our souls but the redemption of every aspect of this entire groaning creation (Rom. 8:22). Through the cross, God reconciles *all things* to himself, "whether things on earth or things in heaven" (Col. 1:20).

In other words, God's salvation is as big as his creation, and in redemption God reaffirms the goodness of creation. And it's precisely on this point that Calvinism—the big, expansive, "complex" Calvinism that Kuyper extols—counters the rampant gnosticism that characterizes North American evangelicalism. As Kuyper succinctly puts it, "Calvinism puts an end once and for all to contempt for the world, neglect of temporal and under-valuation of cosmical things." In Calvinism, "cosmical life has regained its worth not at the expense of things eternal, but by virtue of its capacity as God's handiwork and as a revelation of God's attributes" (119–20). In my own pilgrimage, this has been the signal, prophetic contribution of the Reformed tradition in the contemporary American church: to remind us that God himself announced that creation is "very good" (Gen. 1:31). That's not to deny that the fall hasn't radically and comprehensively marred creation, distorting and perverting it, corrupting and corroding it. But it is precisely this theology of *creation* that animates the "big," wide-angle Reformed understanding of *redemption* as the restoration of the entirety of this good creation. God's glory is served not just by saving souls, but by saving bodies too—hence, the resurrection. Indeed, God's glory is expanded not only in a new heaven but in a new earth. Hence Nicholas Wolterstorff, in his important book *Until Justice and Peace Embrace*, talks about Calvinism as "world-formative" Christianity. Unlike the world-rejecting gnosticism that tends to plague evangelical piety, Calvinism is world-affirming in the sense that it is world-formative—or better, world-*re*formative—laboring to undo the curse and foster *shalom*, which is not a matter of getting to heaven, but of seeing heaven on earth. That would be the answer to our prayer: "Thy kingdom come . . ."

So yes, without question, Calvinism and the Reformed tradition are concerned with salvation. It's just that their vision of salvation is as big as God's affirmation of creation.

In hope,

P.S. If you haven't already gotten sucked into contemporary debates, I should flag that the topic of justification is once again a hotbed of controversy, and a number of new Calvinists have been especially vocal in defending what they take to be the Reformed doctrine of justification against what they call "the new perspective on Paul"—embodied in the work of N. T. Wright (and for the record, it seems to me that Wright's account of justification deeply resonates with covenant theology). We can't get into the details here, but I might suggest, à la Kuyper, that these new Calvinists sound more like Lutherans on this matter. In this regard, Wright himself makes an interesting observation in his new book, *Justification: God's Plan and Paul's Vision*:

> For John Calvin, the Mosaic law was given as the way of life for a people already redeemed. . . . I have often

reflected that if it had been the Reformed view of Paul and the law, rather than the Lutheran one, that had dominated biblical scholarship through the two hundred years since the Enlightenment, not only would the new perspective not have been necessary (or not in the same form), but the polarized debates that have run for the last hundred years, between "participationist" and "juristic" forms of soteriology, would not have been necessary either. Many a good old perspective Calvinist has declared that the best way to understand justification is within the context of "being in Christ": the two need not be played off against one another. (72)

Wright goes on to note just what we've discussed before in terms of God's covenantal relation to his people: "In Calvin and his followers," Wright comments, "the great emphasis is on the single plan of God, the fact that God has not changed his mind. There are plenty of theologians who have suggested that God initially gave people a law to see if they could save themselves that way, and then, finding they could not, decided on a Plan B, namely incarnation and crucifixion and 'justification by faith.' But that is what Calvinism has always rejected" (73).

I might be getting ahead of where you are in noting this, but I have no doubt you've heard rumblings about this debate, and I just wanted to suggest that it might be more complicated than some have suggested.

LETTER XXI

What Are We Saved For?

Dear Jesse,

Sorry for a quick follow-up before even getting your reply, but I meant to make a connection in my last letter and would like to develop it here before I forget.

To rehearse: Kuyper helps us see Calvinism not just as an individually oriented soteriology, but as a complex "world- and life-view" that appreciates the sovereignty of the Creator over *all* creation, and hence the sovereignty of the Redeemer in his concerns for the same. So God's concerns in redemption are as wide as his interests in creation. Creation is not just a stage for the drama of human salvation; rather, God's special relationship to humanity—so intensified in the incarnation—is precisely *for* the rest of creation.

So here's the way I'd like to reframe this: Do you remember talking a while back about the notion of covenant—that God is a promise-making, promise-keeping God? Well, as we emphasized, within the narrative of God's covenant making, our promise breaking, and God's faithful covenant keeping, our salvation hinges on the "new covenant" (Jer. 31:31–34) in which God stipulates the conditions of the covenant, but then the God-man *keeps* that covenant on our behalf and empowers us to finally keep our promises by imparting to us the power of the Holy Spirit (Rom. 8:1–4). But what are the expectations and obligations of the new covenant? Or, to put it more succinctly, what are we saved *for*?

Again, I've been emphasizing we only understand redemption and salvation if we look back to creation. God's redemptive work is about restoration, not addition; salvation is healing what's been corrupted, not adding to what is deficient. In traditional theological terms, the Reformed tradition has always emphasized that grace *restores* nature, not that grace "perfects" or "completes" nature. When the Lord announces, "I am making everything new!" (Rev. 21:5), we can see that God's saving work is a renewal of his creation. It's not salvation *from* creation but the salvation *of* his creation that was pronounced "very good."

So what are we saved *for*? Well, just as creation's redemption is its restoration and renewal, so we are redeemed, renewed, and empowered to finally be able to do what we were *created* for. And what was that? *To be God's image bearers*. Our creational mandate—our mission and task as the pinnacle of God's creation—was precisely the task of bearing God's image. The image of God is not a stamp imprinted on us that makes us somehow look-alikes of God; rather, to be created in God's image is to be commissioned with the task and mission of being God's ambassadors in and for creation, God's emissaries and vice-regents charged with the task of "ruling"—tending and governing creation—which is why the biblical narrative ends, in the book of Revelation, with humanity ruling alongside Christ (Rev. 20:4).

So, we were created to be God's image bearers (Gen. 1:27), and that work and mission of being God's ambassadors is bound up with what is often described as the "cultural mandate" in Genesis: "Be fruitful and multiply, and fill the earth, and subdue it; and rule over the fish of the sea and over the birds of the sky and over every living thing that moves on the earth" (Gen. 1:28 NASB). The way we bear God's image is by tending and cultivating his creation. Did you notice the dynamics there in Genesis 1:26–28? God creates humanity in order to "rule" (v. 26), thus creates humanity in his image (v. 27), and that "ruling" takes the form of being fruitful, filling the earth, and "taking care" of creation. (I love how *The Message* puts this: "Prosper! Reproduce! Fill Earth! Take charge! Be responsible . . .")

I think the best way to understand this creational mission is in terms of "cultivation," in part because it relates to our word for "culture" (which tracks back to a Latin word meaning "to tend"). God places us in creation as his ambassadors and emissaries, but also as co-laborers, entrusting to us the task of unfolding all the potential that's packed into creation. When God calls creation into being, he announces that it's "very good," but he doesn't announce that it's finished! Creation doesn't come into existence ready-made with schools, art museums, and farms; those are all begging to be unpacked. But unfurling that potential is going to take work—and that work is the labor of "culture," of cultivation, of unpacking. Indeed, creation is itself a call and an invitation; the riches and potential of God's good creation are entrusted to his image bearers. That is our calling and commission.

So when God creates the world, he doesn't imagine its end (its *telos*) to be a people just devoted to singing praise songs eternally. God's glory is most multiplied and expanded when all of the rich potential of his creation is unfolded and unpacked into the life-giving institutions that contribute to its flourishing. In a way, you could say that God has commissioned us to be his image bearers in order to help him show off his glory in what he has made. In short, the creational work of culture—unpacking the stores of potential latent in creation "to the praise of his glory"—is what we're made for. And since redemption is precisely the renewal and restoration of creation, then good culture-making is also what we're *saved* for.

If you picture it this way—that is, if you understand it within the grand narrative of salvation history that unfolds in Scripture—then you can see a new connection between the Great Commission (Matt. 28:18–20) and the cultural mandate (Gen. 1:28). The church is that people commissioned to tell the good news of God's salvation precisely in order to announce that God's grace has made it possible for us to take up our vocation as creatures bearing his image. We are the people announcing the new covenant that finally makes it possible for us to fulfill our calling in the original covenant of creation itself.

In fact, you can also think of this in terms of election: what if we thought of creation as the "first" election in a sense? That is, what if we saw humanity being deputized as God's image bearers as the first instance of God's election, which is always an election *to responsibility*? Then, in a similar way, the election of the church is a sort of renewal of that "creational" election and a restoration of that cultural commission. Does that make sense? What I'm trying to appreciate is Kuyper's insight that Calvinism is not just a doctrine of individual salvation; it's an entire "complex" or "world- and life-view" that envisions God's interests more widely than the rescue of souls. I think a careful, comprehensive reading of Scripture bears this out.

Think about it,

P.S. Given the metaphor I've used about "unpacking" or "unfolding" the potential within creation, it's interesting to consider the very opening lines of Kuyper's Princeton lectures, where he sings the praises of the "new world" in America:

> A traveler from the old European Continent, disembarking on the shore of this New World, feels as the Psalmist says, that "His thoughts crowd upon him like a multitude." Compared with the eddying waters of your new stream of life, the old stream in which he was moving seems almost frostbound and dull; and here, on American ground, for the first time, he realizes how so many divine potencies, which were hidden away in the bosom of mankind from our very creation, but which our old world was incapable of developing, are now beginning to disclose their inward splendor, thus promising a still richer store of surprises for the future. (*Calvinism: Six Stone Foundation Lectures*, 9)

Did you hear that? Kuyper thought the American experiment was particularly fruitful in "developing" the "divine potencies" that were "hidden away" in creation. And the entire upshot of his lectures is to explain how Calvinism nourished and propelled this development.

Bibliographical Providence

Dear Jesse,

Very cool that you "happened" across a used copy of Kuyper's *Calvinism* lectures. But of course, you don't really think this was a "coincidence," right? C'mon—we're Calvinists! Actually, I take this really seriously. It might sound corny, even superstitious, but I've always thought of bookstores and libraries as special, almost sacramental places: places where God surprises me, meets me, guides me, and challenges me. So one of my favorite "spiritual" sites in town is the new arrivals shelf at the downtown library. In fact, I consider the new arrivals shelf a kind of Sinai where I go expecting God to show me something: to *reveal* something. In the public library, the acquisitions are not governed by "academic" concerns. There is no logic of selection that I control on the new arrivals shelf. That's why I experience it as a kind of sheer grace, this gift where I encounter books I wouldn't even know to go looking for. And my Calvinism primes me to think that God has *appointments* for me on the new arrivals shelf—that there are surprises and gifts waiting there for me left by the hand of the Creator. Am I crazy?

Actually, this goes back to an early, formative experience for me that I suspect you'll appreciate. As I think I told you, because Deanna and I got married so young, one of our professors counseled us to take a year off school and just work during our first year of marriage—citing Deuteronomy 24:5 just a little out of context, I think, but it was actually wise advice for us (now twenty years into our marriage!). This was after my freshman year of college, and just after my Reformed epiphany, having discovered the Hodges, Warfield, and W. G. T. Shedd. But while taking a year off, working in a factory, we were in a small town without a college or university, let alone a seminary, and so I found myself library-less. All those volumes that were at my fingertips in the college library were now hundreds of miles away, and the budget of a young married couple didn't allow much room for building my own library. Plus, where would I ever find such books? (Not in the local "Christian bookstore," that's for sure!) I was resigned to a fallow year.

Then one day we somehow happened into a tiny little Mennonite bookstore in the village of Tavistock, Ontario. Actually, calling it a "bookstore" might give you the wrong picture. It was more like a mudroom in someone's house with some cards and trinkets on the shelves, a few tracts and booklets, and some Bibles in the corner. I think Deanna was looking for a birthday card, and being a dutiful new husband, I joined the search, poking amongst the trinkets and knickknacks looking for anything to distract my inattention. I found the one shelf of quasi-theological books and was browsing when I noticed a sealed collection of books on the top shelf, coated in dust. The spines looked vaguely familiar, so I stretched to coax them off the shelf in a sputter of dust bunnies.

The three volumes toppled down together because the set was still sealed in cellophane wrap. The covers of the books were a marbled navy-and-azure pattern, a throwback to those gorgeous books produced in the nineteenth century. And inscribed in gold on the black spines were these words: "Dogmatic Theology. W. G. T. Shedd." I'm not kidding.

Of course, this made absolutely no sense whatsoever. What on earth was a brand new, reprint edition of Shedd's trilogy doing in a Mennonite bookstore in a rural Ontario village? I hope it's not selfish, but I have always chalked this up to the gift of providence, and these books became my lifeline during my hiatus from school. Shedd's *Dogmatic Theology* was my curriculum away from college, my personal tutor as I immersed myself in the riches of Reformed theology. It was also in Shedd that I first read of Plato and Aristotle and cut my teeth on philosophy. And I can remember one especially terrible sermon I preached on the Trinity largely because I was just parroting Shedd's chapter on the subject! But those volumes will always have a special place in my heart and memory, and I've yet to give up on the conviction that they weren't there "by accident."

Actually, the books also have another special association for me, not unrelated to something we discussed last time. Having been quickly formed as a good fundamentalist, I had also quickly absorbed the quasi-gnosticism that goes along with it—the sort of "contempt for the world" and for embodiment that Calvinism, as Kuyper emphasized, puts to an end. And one of the outcomes of that gnosticism, with its despising of materiality and embodiment, is also a strangely negative relationship to sexuality (despite all the rhetoric of "family values"). Because all I had ever heard about sex was, "Don't!" I didn't really have a place in my theology for its affirmation. So the abstinence I had been trying to cultivate premaritally also became a marital habit! As a result, late into the evening I would be bent over my desk, surrounded by Shedd's *Dogmatic Theology*, plumbing the depths of Reformed theology while Deanna was falling asleep alone in our bedroom.

Then one night I couldn't find my books. I rifled through the piles on my desk, under my desk, in my closet. I looked on the coffee table, the kitchen table, the end table. Where were my sacred volumes? I stormed into our bedroom with an accusatory question, only to find Deanna there in a negligee from our honeymoon, having draped herself in all three volumes of *Dogmatic Theology*. "Is this what it's going to take to get you to come to bed?" she asked coyly. I've never looked at those books the same way since. Fortunately, not long after this I read Kuyper, who convinced me of the goodness of creation and the redemption of "all things." Four kids later, I'm grateful to have been introduced to wide-angle Calvinism. But I'll always owe a debt of gratitude to W. G. T. Shedd.

Whimsically yours, in all seriousness,

LETTER XXIII

Enjoying God by Enjoying Creation

Dear Jesse,

Sorry I got so carried away with my theory of "bibliographical providence" that I forgot to answer your question! Let me try to tackle it here.

It is true that I sketched an understanding of the "end" (or *telos*) of humanity that seems to differ a bit from the Westminster Catechism, and hence from Piper's gloss on that. But maybe not. Let's think through this.

So the Shorter Catechism opens with that provocative question, "What is the chief end of man?" It's a great question precisely because it's a *teleological* question: it gets us thinking about who we are in terms of what we're meant for, in terms of our *telos* or goal. I love it. It's a kind of stretched sense of our identity that defines us by our future, by what we're called to be. There's a whole eschatology crammed into that little question.

And the answer is, I think, equally marvelous: "To glorify God and enjoy him forever." You'll no doubt hear the heart and soul of Jonathan Edwards's ministry compressed into that answer. Indeed. But I also hear St. Augustine in that "enjoy." As he articulates it in *Teaching Christianity*, what we love is what we enjoy. So insofar as we've been created to love God ("You have made us for yourself, and our *hearts* are restless until they rest in you," *Confessions*, 1.1.1), we are ultimately called to *enjoy* God. That "enjoy" runs counter to all the caricatures of the Puritans laden in our adjective "puritanical." Given how dour and dreary Calvinists can sometimes be, the catechism is a wonderful reminder that the good news of grace is bound up with joy and delight, not the grumpy observation of a set of rules. God created us for joy. As you know, John Piper's (Edwardsean) tweak on this is fabulous: we glorify God *by* enjoying him forever.

Now, my Kuyperian rendition of Calvinism is certainly different in this respect, insofar as this wide-angle version of Calvinism feels a bit "bigger" than the more narrow concern with my personal salvation that seems to characterize some forms of Calvinism. However, I don't think there's a necessary tension with the Shorter Catechism on this point. In fact, what if, in the spirit of Piper, I tried out my own Augustinian/Kuyperian gloss on the first question of the catechism? On that rendering, the answer to the question, "What is the chief end of man?" might be: "To glorify God by enjoying his creation forever." Or better, "To glorify God and enjoy him by enjoying his creation forever."

Before you get worried that this is too "worldly" (though there might not be a more "worldly" theologian than John Calvin!), let me try to unpack this within an Augustinian framework. (You might want to find a comfy seat; when I get started on Augustine, I tend to get carried away!)

I've emphasized that one of the intuitions of Calvinism is actually an affirmation of the goodness of creation (Gen. 1:31). While recognizing the brokenness and fallenness of creation, Calvin and his heirs recognized that this was a corruption of a good creation, not a feature of creation as such. And they were primed to see this precisely because they were so influenced by Augustine (as I suggested a while back, the Reformation is really an Augustinian renewal movement). For Augustine, anything that's created has to be good because only the good Creator can actually create, that is, bring something out of nothing. So anything that exists owes its existence to the gift of a good, creating God—a kind of "creative grace," you might say. Or, to put it otherwise, the devil can't create a thing. He can only corrupt and corrode. "Evil," then, is always and only parasitic upon the good—evil is the cowardly nothingness that eats away at God's productive goodness (which is why good *has* to precede evil).

The upshot is this: creation—and the *matter* of creation, the material stuff that makes up creation—is not inherently evil or fallen. Indeed creation, insofar as it is called into existence by God's creative love, is fundamentally *good*. However, this is not some kind of blank check for the world, nor does it have anything to do with the soppy, Oprah-like tripe that suggests "everyone is basically good" (this is Augustine we're talking about, after all—that's exactly the nonsense he heard coming from the Pelagians). Indeed, no one was more attentive to the temptations and idolatries of "the world" than Augustine. The bulk of his *Confessions* is a long meditation on 1 John 2:15–17: "Do not love the world nor the things in the world. If anyone loves the world, the love of the Father is not in him. For all that is in the world, the lust of the flesh and the lust of the eyes and the boastful pride of life, is not from the Father, but is from the world. The world is passing away, and also its lusts; but the one who does the will of God lives forever" (NASB). But for Augustine, "the world" and "creation" are not synonymous. In fact, you might say that the world is our own making—in a way, the world is what our disordered wills have made of creation. The world is that disordered system that is the fruit of fallen, sinful human beings engaging in bad culture making.

The temptations of the world, then, are not so much a reflection of what's wrong with creation; they are an indicator of what's wrong with us. What's at issue here is not creation per se, but how we *relate* to creation. For Augustine, sin is a matter of *how*, not *what*. "Things" aren't sinful; what's sinful is how we *relate* to them, what we *do* with them. And this comes down to a matter of what we *love* and how we love.

Let's take an example like sexuality (which I know is always kind of a "live" issue for young folks): obviously the 1 John passage lists the "lust of the flesh" as among the temptations of "the world." Does that mean that bodies are bad? That sex is bad? That erotic attraction is bad? No. Remember, the same God that commissioned us as his image bearers also exhorted us to "be fruitful and multiply." So it's not embodiment or sex that's the problem. God is not out to save us *from* our bodies (in which case, the resurrection of *the body* would be a strange strategy). Rather, what's at issue is how we relate to our bodies (and the bodies of others!). What needs to change, Augustine says, is not the stuff of creation but our *love*.

So Augustine introduces an important distinction (you can see this across his entire corpus, but especially in book 1 of *Teaching Christianity*): what God desires and designs for his creatures is a "right order of love," which simply means that we are created and called to be creatures who ultimately love the Triune God, and thus find our identity and delight in that rightly ordered love. For Augustine, we are what we love. In fact, we can't stop loving: even fallen, sinful humanity is still propelled to love; but as sinners, we love the wrong things in the wrong way. We end up, in the words of a great old Waylon Jennings song, "lookin' for love in all the wrong places." (In fact, if you look at the lyrics of that song, it almost reads like an Augustinian praise chorus.) We can't stop looking for love (U2's entire discography is a meditation on this Augustinian point). But only by God's grace can that impulsion to love be rightly ordered, rightly directed to God himself. By the grace of God, our love can find the end point it was created for: God himself. This sounds like Jonathan Edwards, doesn't it?

Now, it is this "right order" of love that helps us understand how to relate to God's good creation. And here's where Augustine's distinction between "use" and "enjoyment" comes into play. ("Enjoy"—get it? Shorter Catechism, anyone?) Augustine's point is this: we are created to love God above all else, as our *ultimate* love. And for Augustine, what I love and what I "enjoy" are synonymous. In fact, if I want to know what you ultimately love, I just have to look at what you ultimately enjoy—what makes you happy. (Augustine, unlike many Calvinists, is not afraid to say that God wants us to be happy!) Since the Creator has made us for himself, our hearts will be restless and anxious and disappointed if they don't ultimately love and enjoy God.

OK, but where does *creation* fit into this picture? Does creation just kind of fall away? Do the "things of this world become strangely dim" when I love God? Not for Augustine. Rather, he would say that while I am called to *enjoy* God, God's good creation can then be received as a gift to be *used*. In other words, I *use* the creation as a means of *enjoying* God. This also helps Augustine diagnose what's wrong with "the world" of 1 John 2:15–17: creation becomes "the world" precisely when we love creation *instead of* the Creator (cf. Rom. 1:21–23). When that happens, I make an idol of creation by enjoying it rather than using it. But when I love and enjoy God, it's not like I abandon creation; rather, I will relate to it properly. I will "use" it as a means of enjoying God.

It's as if, once your love is rightly ordered, you get all of creation back again, a gift given by God *to* enjoy him. The things that constitute the temptations of "the world" are repositioned and recontextualized, in a sense, so that "the world" can once again be received *as* creation. In fact, within this context of rightly ordered love, Augustine so wants to affirm the goodness of God's creation that he sort of fudges his own distinction a little bit and says that those who rightly love the Creator can use the creation "with delight," and even "enjoy" creation in a sense (*Teaching Christianity* 1.33). You might think of this as a distinction between lowercase-*e* and capital-*E* "enjoyment": when, by grace, our love is rightly ordered so that we Enjoy God, then we'll realize that God gives us his creation so that we can Enjoy him. But when our love is ordered, we can then *enjoy* creation as the means of *Enjoying* God. And so you get my little gloss on the Shorter Catechism: "What is the chief end of man?" "To glorify God and Enjoy him by enjoying his creation forever."

Well, the length of this letter might indicate that you're now too advanced for letters! You don't need my little missives anymore; you can just dive right into the books we've been discussing. I will say that Augustine's *Teaching Christianity*, like the *Confessions*, is one of my "desert island books." (I have to confess I think I'd take both of them before the *Institutes*. ☺) If you're looking for a place to start your "Reformed" education, you couldn't do much better than that.

Love,

Acknowledgments

My initial vision for *Letters to a Young Calvinist* arose from the conflation of two strange bedfellows. First, back in 2003, I read Christopher Hitchens's *Letters to a Young Contrarian*. (This was back when Hitchens was a scathing political critic and illuminating literary critic—before he hitched his wagon to the secular fundamentalism of the new atheism.) Shortly after that, I read George Weigel's masterful articulation of "the Catholic difference" in his *Letters to a Young Catholic*. In both cases, I found the epistolary form engaging and helpful, and I started imagining what has now become this book.

But the more existential impetus for this little pastoral volume is friendships I forged while living in Los Angeles, directing the college and career ministry of a Pentecostal church in Hawthorne, California, and teaching at a Catholic university perched over Marina del Rey. This was certainly not the most likely seedbed for Calvinism to take root. And yet these young people, hungry for theological depth and an intellectual tradition, welcomed the Reformed tradition as a breath of fresh air. They had many questions. Some of these letters capture our actual conversations, but all of them were written with these friends in mind. And so I'm very happy to dedicate the book to them, with gratitude for their friendship and hope that their *love* might abound more and more, so that they can discern what really matters (Phil. 1:9–10).

I'm grateful to John Witvliet and Todd Cioffi for letting me think out loud with them at an early stage of the project. Jim Bratt generously shared with me some chapters of his forthcoming biography of Abraham Kuyper, which helped me to crystallize some later themes in the book. And in a way, I felt like Rich Mouw was always at my side—or ahead of me—as I worked on this series of letters, which are, I hope, "Mouwish" in spirit. As always, Bob Hosack, Jeremy Wells, Brian Bolger, Caitlin MacKenzie, and all the good folks at Brazos were both encouraging and patient. I'm grateful for our ongoing partnership. Finally, my thanks to the

Sparrows for bottomless cups of coffee and a hospitable space for writing in the neighborhood.

I like to suggest that my books have a kind of soundtrack. While working on this book, it was most often Bach's Cello Suites that were playing in the background. This seemed especially appropriate given what Cal Stapert has shown to be the "Reformedness" of Bach's musical theology (in his marvelous book *My Only Comfort: Death, Deliverance, and Discipleship in the Music of Bach*). The deep throaty growl of the cello seems to be owning up to the heavy brokenness of creation, but the light dance of this same instrument helps us imagine the world otherwise. Perhaps it's this tension and hope that also had me listening to Ryan Adams's *Heartbreaker* along the way.

Bibliography

Augustine. *City of God*. Translated by Henry Bettenson. Hammondsworth, UK: Penguin, 1984.

————. *Confessions*. Translated by Henry Chadwick. Oxford: Oxford University Press, 1992.

————. *Teaching Christianity* [*De doctrina christiana*]. Translated by Edmund Hill. New York: New City Press, 1996.

Bouwsma, William J. *John Calvin: A Sixteenth Century Portrait*. Oxford: Oxford University Press, 1988.

Bunyan, John. *The Pilgrim's Progress*. Hammondsworth, UK: Penguin, 2004.

Calvin, John. *Institutes of the Christian Religion* [1559]. Edited by John T. McNeill. Translated by Ford Lewis Battles. Philadelphia: Westminster/John Knox, 1960.

—————. *The Letters of John Calvin: Selected from the Bonnet Edition*. Edinburgh: Banner of Truth, 1980.

Clapp, Rodney. "The Sin of Winnie-the-Pooh." *Christianity Today*, November 9, 1992, 29–32.

Colson, Charles, with Nancy Pearcey. *How Now Shall We Live?* Wheaton: Tyndale, 1999.

Ecumenical Creeds and Reformed Confessions. Grand Rapids: Faith Alive, 1988.

Frame, John M. "Machen's Warrior Children." In *Alister E. McGrath and Evangelical Theology: A Dynamic Engagement*, edited by Sung Wook Chung, 113–46. Grand Rapids: Baker Academic, 2003.

Hansen, Collin. *Young, Restless, Reformed: A Journalist's Journey with the New Calvinists*. Wheaton: Crossway, 2008.

Hitchens, Christopher. *Letters to a Young Contrarian*. New York: Basic Books, 2001.

Horton, Michael. *A Better Way: Re-discovering the Drama of God-centered Worship*. Grand Rapids: Baker Books, 2003.

—————. *Covenant and Eschatology: The Divine Drama*. Louisville: Westminster John Knox, 2002.

—————. *Introducing Covenant Theology*. Grand Rapids: Baker Books, 2009.

Joo, Seung-Joong, and Kyeong-Jin Kim. "The Reformed Tradition in Korea." In *The Oxford History of Christian Worship*, edited by Geoffrey Wainwright and Karen Westfield Tucker, 484–91. Oxford: Oxford University Press, 2006.

Kuyper, Abraham. *Calvinism: Six Stone Foundation Lectures*. Grand Rapids: Eerdmans, 1943.

———. "Sphere Sovereignty." In *Abraham Kuyper: A Centennial Reader*. Edited by James D. Bratt. Grand Rapids: Eerdmans, 1998.

Lane, Anthony N. S. *John Calvin: Student of the Church Fathers*. Edinburgh: T&T Clark, 1999.

Lewis, C. S. *The Screwtape Letters*. San Francisco: HarperOne, 2001.

MacIntyre, Alasdair. *After Virtue*. 2nd ed. Notre Dame: University of Notre Dame Press, 1984.

Marsden, George. *Jonathan Edwards: A Life*. New Haven: Yale University Press, 2004.

———. *A Short Life of Jonathan Edwards*. Grand Rapids: Eerdmans, 2008.

Mathison, Keith A. *Given for You: Reclaiming Calvin's Doctrine of the Lord's Supper*. Phillipsburg, NJ: P&R, 2002.

McGrath, Alister. *Christianity's Dangerous Idea: The Protestant Revolution—A History from the Sixteenth Century to the Twenty-First*. San Francisco: HarperOne, 2008.

Mouw, Richard. *Calvinism in the Las Vegas Airport*. Grand Rapids: Zondervan, 2004.

———. *When the Kings Come Marching In: Isaiah and the New Jerusalem*. Rev. ed. Grand Rapids: Eerdmans, 2002.

Mueenuddin, Daniyal. *In Other Rooms, Other Wonders*. New York: W. W. Norton, 2009.

Muller, Richard. *Post-Reformation Dogmatics: The Rise and Development of Reformed Orthodoxy*. 4 vols. Grand Rapids: Baker Academic, 2003.

———. *The Unaccommodated Calvin: Studies in the Foundation of a Theological Tradition*. Oxford: Oxford University Press, 2000.

Noll, Mark. *The Princeton Theology, 1812–1921: Scripture, Science, and Theological Method from Archibald Alexander to Benjamin Warfield*. Grand Rapids: Baker Academic, 2001.

Packer, J. I. *A Quest for Godliness: The Puritan Vision of the Christian Life*. Wheaton: Crossway, 1994.

Piper, John. *Desiring God: Meditations of a Christian Hedonist*. Eugene, OR: Multnomah, 1987.

———. *God's Passion for His Glory: Living the Vision of Jonathan Edwards*. Wheaton: Crossway, 2006.

Poythress, Vern. *Understanding Dispensationalists*. 2nd ed. Phillipsburg, NJ: P&R, 1994.

Schiller, Freidrich. *On the Aesthetic Education of Man in a Series of Letters*. Edited by E. M. Wilkinson and L. A. Willoughby. Oxford: Oxford University Press, 1983.

Shedd, William G. T. *Dogmatic Theology*. Nashville: Thomas Nelson, 1980.

Smith, James K. A. *Desiring the Kingdom: Worship, Worldview, and Cultural Formation*. Grand Rapids: Baker Academic, 2009.

———. *The Devil Reads Derrida: And Other Essays on the University, the Church, Politics, and the Arts*. Grand Rapids: Eerdmans, 2009.

———. *Thinking in Tongues: Pentecostal Contributions to Christian Philosophy.* Grand Rapids: Eerdmans, 2010.

Sproul, R. C. *Thy Brother's Keeper.* Brentwood, TN: Wolgemuth and Hyatt, 1988.

Stapert, Calvin. *My Only Comfort: Death, Deliverance, and Discipleship in the Music of Bach.* Grand Rapids: Eerdmans, 2000.

Steinmetz, David. *Luther in Context.* 2nd ed. Grand Rapids: Baker Academic, 2002.

Van Biema, David. "The New Calvinism," *Time*, March 12, 2009.

Warfield, B. B., *Augustine and Calvin.* Phillipsburg, NJ: P&R, 1956.

———. *Studies in Theology.* Edinburgh: Banner of Truth, 1988.

Weigel, George. *Letters to a Young Catholic.* New York: Basic Books, 2004.

Williams, D. H. *Evangelicals and Tradition: The Formative Influence of the Early Church.* Grand Rapids: Baker Academic, 2005.

Witte, John, Jr. *The Reformation of Rights: Law, Religion, and Human Rights in Early Modern Calvinism.* Cambridge: Cambridge University Press, 2007.

Wolterstorff, Nicholas. *Until Justice and Peace Embrace.* Grand Rapids: Eerdmans, 1983.

Wright, N. T. *Justification: God's Plan and Paul's Vision.* Downers Grove, IL: InterVarsity, 2009.

Zachman, Randall C., ed. *John Calvin and Roman Catholicism: Critique and Engagement, Then and Now.* Grand Rapids: Baker Academic, 2008.

———. *John Calvin as Teacher, Pastor, and Theologian: The Shape of His Writings and Thought.* Grand Rapids: Baker Academic, 2006.